BUY THE MILK FIRST

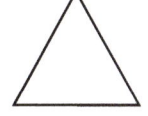

... AND OTHER SECRETS TO FINANCIAL
PROSPERITY, REGARDLESS OF YOUR INCOME

MURRAY J LEE

One Printers Way
Altona, MB R0G 0B0
Canada

www.friesenpress.com

Copyright © 2022 by Murray J Lee, CPA
First Edition — 2022

All rights reserved.

No part of this publication may be reproduced in any form, or by any means, electronic or mechanical, including photocopying, recording, or any information browsing, storage, or retrieval system, without permission in writing from FriesenPress.

ISBN
978-1-03-912205-5 (Hardcover)
978-1-03-912204-8 (Paperback)
978-1-03-912206-2 (eBook)

1. Business & Economics, Personal Finance, Money Management

Distributed to the trade by The Ingram Book Company

ABOUT THE TITLE

When my parents were newly married, they were extremely poor. Although they were blessed with a baby girl, they had no money. My dad was going to school full time during the day, and he worked as a custodian at night. They were always worried that their money would run out before the month did. So, at the end of each month, when my dad was paid, my parents had two priorities. First, they paid the rent for the next month. Second, they went out and bought enough milk for my sister to make sure she had enough food for the month. If they were going to run out of food, my mom and dad figured they would go hungry, but they were never going to let their baby girl go hungry. Although they had lots of expenses (including food for themselves), they understood the rules of prioritization. Their highest priority was their daughter, and they made sure that their limited money went first to providing a roof over her head and second to buying food for her to eat. In other words, they made sure to "Buy the Milk First". All other expenses were a lower priority. There were months when the money did run out before the month did, but their baby girl never suffered.

We all have a long list of activities we would like to do or items we would like to acquire. We also have limited resources and therefore lack the ability to do or acquire all the things on our list. How then do we best resolve this dilemma?

This book was written to answer that question. It is full of financial wisdom, principles and personal stories that will help you to answer that question, to master your finances and to generate wealth. It will show you how to make sure that you too "Buy the Milk First".

A NOTE FROM THE AUTHOR

The purpose of this book is to help people improve their personal finances. In fact, I originally wrote this book to help my children and grandchildren improve their personal finances. However, as I worked on the book and spoke with others, I quickly realised that an improved knowledge and application of personal financial principles would greatly benefit most people. The proper application of sound financial principles will help people avoid the much too frequent and unnecessary suffering and potentially devastating impact of financial stress, and to secure financial prosperity, happiness, and independence. This is why I also created the website www.buythemilkfirst.com. The book will help explain the principles, the website will help in applying those principles. If you are like my children and grandchildren and just starting out in your financial life, if you were not taught personal finance in school, or if you are simply experiencing financial hardships, this book, and the website I created, is for you. I know the financial principles outlined in this book and reinforced in the website can help you.

~Murray J. Lee~

CONTENTS

Preface   v

PART I
UNDERSTANDING MONEY

1: Wealth Is Not a Number	3
2: The Law of the Harvest	5
3: Natural Laws Can Be neither Broken nor Cheated	9
4: Sleep When the Wind Blows	13

PART II
CREATING THE PLAN

5: Plan Your Financial Future	19
6: Own Your Mistakes	23
7: Plan for the Worst, Hope for the Best	25

PART III
PRIORITIZING THE PLAN

8: A Four-Letter Word for Freedom	31
9: The Is and the Is Not	33
10: Buy the Milk First	37
11: The Rule of Financial Happiness	39
12: Doing What You Want with What You Got	47
13: Help! I Am Short of Funds	51
14: Debt: The Good, the Bad, and the Ugly	55
15: Help! I Am Already in Debt	63

PART IV
PERFORMING THE PLAN

16: The Dynamic Duo—The Secrets to Wealth Creation	73
17: Your Financial Personal Flotation Device	83
18: The Four "Do" Laws of Investing	89
19: The Four "Do Not" Laws of Investing	95
20: Business Relationships: How to Choose Them, How to Keep Them	101
21: Retirement: Are You Financially Ready?	105

PART V
PASSING ON THE PLAN

22: Lending to Family and Friends	111
23: Money Is Only a Symbol	115
24: Money Can Buy Happiness	117
25: Conclusion	119
Appendix I: Summary of Key Takeaways	123
About the Author	129

PREFACE

It was early 1982, and I was an intern at a small accounting firm. It was then, early in my career, when I had a conversation with a client of the firm that stuck with me my entire life. The client was the wife of a dentist—a man with a good practice and a good income. Yet, despite their strong income, this family was always having financial problems—so much so that they had to hire an accounting firm to manage their personal finances. One day while on the phone with the client, she said to me that she did not understand how her husband could have such a good income, and yet the family still had financial problems. I have never forgotten the despair in her voice and the conversation we had.

That conversation was perhaps the genesis of this book. And that family exemplifies why this book is needed because, despite their good income, they had never learned how to effectively manage their finances, and that failure was negatively impacting their lives. Fast-forward several years to when I was contemplating writing this book, and I was having a conversation with a couple of my children about how education systems are failing with respect to teaching financial literacy. Our education system excels at training students to be great professionals, whether it is teachers, engineers, doctors, or accountants. We are also great at training students to work in the trades, such as plumbers and electricians. We work hard to prepare people to be able to work and earn an income. Unfortunately, we fail to teach people what to do once they have earned an income. We fail to teach people how to manage their finances and how to enjoy life, yet this is arguably the most important skill set they need.

Our failure to properly teach people how to manage their finances has resulted in an immeasurable amount of unnecessary grief and stress. As a degreed and certified accountant with over 35 years' experience, I have witnessed lots of misery and tears, all resulting from people's lack of ability to effectively manage the resources they have worked so hard to earn. Thus, I was not surprised when I came across a 2015 study on stress in America by the American Psychological Association. The study found that nearly three-quarters (72%) of adults reported feeling stressed about money at least some of the time and that 64% of adults say money is a somewhat or a very significant source of stress. Sadly, stress about money significantly reduces our quality of life, our happiness, and even our health. What's even sadder is that for most people, all this stress is unnecessary.

When I see the pain and suffering that is created by a lack of financial literacy, two things happen. First, my heart breaks for those who needlessly suffer. Second, I become stressed as I worry about my own children and grandchildren, and I wonder whether they will have the financial literacy to avoid all that unnecessary stress and pain.

I originally wrote this book to benefit my children and grandchildren. As they start out on their financial lives, I hope to provide them with some basic financial wisdom. I hope to give them counsel that will bless their lives and help them successfully navigate the financial jungle. I hope to lead them on a journey and help them to discover the secrets that will lead them to a life of financial prosperity. I know that if they read and apply the financial principles discussed in this book, they will not only avoid the unnecessary suffering and potentially devastating impact of financial stress, but they will also secure financial prosperity, happiness, and independence, regardless of their income.

If you are like my children and grandchildren and just starting out in your financial life, if you were not taught personal finance in school, or if you are simply experiencing financial hardships, this book is for you. I know the financial principles outlined in this book can help you.

The concepts discussed in this book are basic financial laws that must be obeyed to achieve any form of financial success. They are the concepts that, back in 1982, would have well served my client: the dentist's family.

To my children and grandchildren, I have no hesitation in promising you that if you apply these financial principles, you will lead a happier and more fulfilled life. If others—besides my children and grandchildren—choose to read this book, I have no hesitation in making you the same promise. All those who are seeking prosperity and hoping to improve their financial situation can learn and apply these principles to benefit their lives.

Here's to a financially stress-free life!

PART I

UNDERSTANDING MONEY

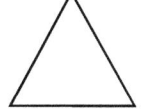

1

WEALTH IS NOT A NUMBER

Most people want to build wealth, but they do not really know what wealth means, and therefore they cannot really build it. A financial institution recently ran an ad of people walking around with numbers over their heads. In this ad, they constantly asked the question, "What is your number?" What they were getting at is, how much money do you need so you can retire? What is your number? Personally, I think that an ad like that, from a financial entity, demonstrated a lack of understanding of what true financial success is. I know that it was marketing, but that kind of marketing leads to financial misinformation. It trains people to think that financial success, or wealth, is defined as a certain amount of money or a "number." But I think there is a better way to define financial success—a way that results in much less stress.

Financial success should not be defined by money, but rather by time. Ask yourself this simple question: If I quit working today, how long could I live and maintain my current lifestyle? If you have enough resources to cover six months of expenses, then you are six-months wealthy. If you could live a year on your current resources, then you are one-year wealthy. If you could maintain your current lifestyle indefinitely based on your current resources, then you are independently wealthy. This is the stage all of us should seek to achieve, as this is the stage where we have true financial freedom. This is the stage where we can be free from financial stress.

The time—or the "number"—will be different for each person, as each person has or prefers a different lifestyle. Thus, by defining wealth by time, as opposed to money, you are customizing wealth to each individual person.

Now, I can hear you say, *but time is still a number*. Well, not really. See, if you have passive income—income that you receive, regardless of your labour—and that passive income exceeds your expenses, then you are free. Your number does not matter. Once your resources allow you to maintain your lifestyle, you are independently wealthy. Sure, you can always wish you had a nicer car, a bigger home, etc. But if you think in terms of time and not money, you will be able to sleep when the financial winds blow, you will have less stress, and you will lead a better life.

However, note that I talked about maintaining "your current lifestyle." Lifestyle plays a secondary, but important factor in defining wealth. If I am willing to adjust my lifestyle, then my desired wealth is adjusted, as the amount of funds needed to maintain my lifestyle is adjusted. If your financial goal is to live like a hermit in some hut in the middle of nowhere, and you achieve that, then you are as wealthy as the billionaire with their own private jet flying around the world. Why? Because you both have all the resources you need to do everything you want. Anything more than that is wasted.

So, define wealth first in terms of time and second in terms of lifestyle. This is a more accurate and less stressful approach than defining wealth by money.

Now that you know to identify wealth, first in terms of time—not money—and second in terms of lifestyle, you are ready to start building. What are you building? You are building true financial freedom, as defined by time. You are building a life free from financial stress and worries. You are building the comfort that comes from knowing that you will always have a roof over your head, food on your table, and time to spend on things that you consider the most important. What this means is: do not focus your thoughts and efforts on the size of your bank account, rather focus your thoughts and efforts on the length of time that your assets can maintain your desired lifestyle.

To me, this is true wealth.

KEY TAKEAWAY:
1. **Wealth is defined first by time—not money—and second by lifestyle.**

2

THE LAW OF THE HARVEST

A key step in achieving true wealth is to understand and apply the law of the harvest. Every farmer understands and applies the law of the harvest. The law of the harvest is analogous to our personal finances, and if we understand and apply this law, it can help us carefully plan and thus enable us to have greater financial success. Let me lay out some basic principles for a successful harvest.

1. *If you don't sow, you don't reap*

    This seems rather obvious. If you do not sow the seeds, you cannot expect to harvest. Yet somehow, people think this fundamental law of nature does not apply to them. They expect to get positive results without putting in the effort to generate such results. I have yet to see or hear of a farmer who had a bountiful harvest without first sowing the seeds. It is the same with your personal finances; if you do not sow, you do not reap. Too many people seem to think that the world or the government owes them a living. The world does not owe you anything. A farmer looking at a barren field does not get depressed, nor does he expect the field to somehow get magically planted. A farmer sees a barren field and sees opportunity; he then gets to work and sows the field. It is the same with us and our personal finances. All of us have a barren field. We can choose to see the opportunity and start sowing, or we can wait for the field to be magically sown all by itself. However, if you choose to wait and not sow, do not complain when there is no harvest.

2. *You reap only what has been sown*

This, too, seems rather obvious. Everyone knows that in nature if you plant wheat you are going to harvest wheat. If you want to harvest corn, you'd better not plant wheat— you'd better plant corn. It is no different in the world of personal finance. If you don't plant the right financial seeds—the ones that will produce the personal financial results that you want—then you won't get the desired harvest; and if you don't plant anything, you won't get any harvest. Too many people think that they can plant the seeds of poor financial management and decisions today and yet still reap a harvest of wealth and financial independence tomorrow. It will not happen. For example, spending more than you earn never has and never will create wealth. Planting seeds of poor financial management today can never yield an abundant harvest tomorrow. This defies natural laws that cannot be broken. The later chapters in this book will show you how to plant the seeds of wealth and financial independence today so that you can reap the harvest of wealth and financial independence tomorrow.

3. *You reap in a different season than you sow*

Every farmer knows that you do not plant and reap in the same season. It takes time for the fruits of the labour to be made manifest. You must do all the right things today and then be patient for tomorrow. Patience is the key. In the world of personal finance, too many people have an "I want it now" attitude. They do not understand this very simple law: You reap in a different season than you sow. As a result, in an effort to accelerate the harvest, they make poor decisions that ruin the harvest, such as going into debt.

Young couples often see what their parents have, and they want it now. They need to understand that their parents are living in a different season. Parents are now living in the financial fall of their lives, while the children are living in the financial spring of their lives. Now, because of a lack of patience and a lack of understanding this fundamental law, they start sowing noxious seeds (such as debt) in hopes of being able to harvest right away. (This is a classic failure to plan and failure to prioritize which is more fully discussed later in the book.) But the laws of nature cannot be overcome. As a result of sowing noxious seeds, come harvest time, they will harvest noxious weeds. Sowing noxious seeds today—in hopes of violating this law and reaping in the same season that we sow—will inevitably only lead to a harvest of noxious weeds filled with stress, pain, and financial servitude.

Be patient. Do not try to overcome the law of reaping in a different season than you sow. This inevitably leads to bad decisions and the sowing of noxious weeds, which always leads to a noxious harvest.

4. *You reap more than you sow*

This is another wonderful law that we need to understand. A farmer knows that for every seed planted, he can harvest manyfold, perhaps a hundred-fold or more. If we plant good seeds in the spring, then in the fall we will harvest manyfold what we planted. Unfortunately, the same is also true if we plant bad seeds or noxious seeds. This is why bad financial decisions early in our life are compounded, and the impact on us becomes much bigger later in our life. Good or bad, we will reap manyfold what we plant. On a personal finance side, understanding this law should help motivate us to make good decisions today, knowing that we will reap manyfold tomorrow.

5. *There is a direct correlation between the size of the harvest and the size of the effort*

The more seeds we sow, the greater the harvest. Further, even if we sow an abundance of great seeds in the spring, but we abandon the field and fail to keep working, the harvest will diminish. After a farmer sows, he still needs to water, fertilize, and weed the crop. He needs to continue to protect and nurture the crop. If he lets up in any of these areas, it will directly impact the size of the harvest. So, similarly in personal finance, even if we plant an abundance of good seeds in the spring, but we fail to persevere, and we fail to diligently tend to the crop, the harvest will not be near as abundant as it could have been. We still need to perform.

KEY TAKEAWAYS:
Remember the Law of the Harvest:
1. **If you don't sow, you don't reap.**
2. **You reap only what has been sown.**
3. **You reap in a different season than you sow.**
4. **You reap more than you sow.**
5. **There is a direct correlation between the size of the harvest and the size of the effort.**

3

NATURAL LAWS CAN BE NEITHER BROKEN NOR CHEATED

When I was a young boy, my dad bought our family a pool table for Christmas. Playing on that pool table was when I first became familiar with Newton's third law of motion: "For every action, there is an equal and opposite reaction." This rule applied every time I hit a shot, whether it was using the cue ball to hit another ball, or whether it was trying to bank a shot off the cushion. Every time a ball hit another object, there was always an equal and opposite reaction. The better I became at applying this law, the better pool player I became.

I quickly learned that no matter what I did or how hard I tried, this basic law applied. I could not change it. I could not overcome it. I could not avoid it.

The same applies to your financial life. Try as you may, you cannot change the financial laws, you cannot overcome the financial laws, and you cannot avoid the financial laws. What you can do, though, is learn how to manage and apply financial laws such that they generate the results you want. There are many financial laws, and each law has a different but natural consequence. Those who achieve financial success have learned to understand and apply the financial laws upon which financial success is predicated.

A financial law, understood and kept, will result in financial benefits. A broken financial law will always result in financial loss or pain. What this means is that if you are seeking financial prosperity, you must first learn the financial laws upon which such prosperity is predicated. However, knowledge of financial laws is not enough. Once you have learned the financial laws upon which financial success is predicated, you must then convert your financial knowledge into financial wisdom.

Financial wisdom is derived from three elements. All three must be present to possess financial wisdom.

1. **Knowledge**: We must know the financial laws.
2. **Consequences**: Knowing a financial law and being able to cite a law from memory is not enough. We must understand and be able to anticipate the financial consequences of keeping or breaking a financial law.
3. **Application**: Knowing a financial law and understanding the consequences that arise from that law will accomplish nothing unless we can apply that law to our lives. Application of the law means acting. Knowledge without action is worthless. Knowledge combined with action is priceless.

Thus, financial wisdom is the product of applying the knowledge of financial laws with the understanding of the consequences of those laws.

What this means for you is that to achieve prosperity, you must first learn the laws upon which prosperity is predicated. Second, you must learn to anticipate the positive outcomes that arise from keeping those laws. Third, you must act. You must apply those laws to your personal situation. All three steps are needed. I have seen many people try to break these laws. The only thing that ended up broke was them.

In the chapters that follow, I will talk about many different financial laws and the positive consequences that arise from obeying those financial laws. I will also discuss how to apply the laws to your own situation so that you can reap the financial benefits that arise from keeping those laws.

Remember, the financially wise have learned the following:

1. Financial laws are irrevocable—the same as the laws of physics.
2. The consequences of each individual financial law
3. How to anticipate the consequences of each financial law

4. How to apply the financial laws to create the natural consequences desired

If you read and apply the concepts in this book, you, too, will possess financial wisdom.

KEY TAKEAWAYS:
1. **Financial laws, like natural laws, can be neither broken nor cheated.**
2. **Financial wisdom is the product of applying the knowledge of financial laws with the understanding of the consequences of those laws.**

4

SLEEP WHEN THE WIND BLOWS

If we are going to talk about obtaining financial success, we must first understand what that means. Everybody has a different definition of success. Some people define success by money. Others define success by health, family, or career satisfaction. For the purposes of this book, we will simply define success as the achievement of your objectives, whether they be financial or otherwise.

It is often said that there are three types of people in this world: those who make things happen, those who watch things happen, and those who wonder what happened. Those who make things happen are those who are successful. They make things happen because they set out to accomplish something, and they achieve it. They achieved their objective, and so, in their mind, they are successful.

People achieve success in various ways, but all those who achieve success, in whatever way they define it, have one thing in common. They all apply the 3 Ps of success: Plan, Prioritize, and Perform. And all those who are successful apply the 3 Ps in the correct order. Whether it be in athletics, in business, in the arts, or in any other field, success follows those who correctly plan, prioritize, and perform.

Think of building a house. The first thing you need to do is visualize what you are hoping to build. How big will it be? What kind of rooms will it have? Where will it be situated? Perhaps you even engage an architect or a drafting technician to draw up the plans, carefully thinking through all the things you will need to bring your house to fruition. The more carefully you plan, the less likely it is you will make mistakes, and the easier it will be to achieve your goal. To have "success." Once you create your plan, you will need to prioritize the action steps within the plan. Doing things in the correct order is critical.

For example, we know it is important to install the drywall, but this step must only be done after the electrical and plumbing are done. While all three of those tasks are critically important, doing them out of order will result in chaos and failure. No successful builder ever put the roof on before building the foundation. Thus, establishing the priority is important. Finally, after having made a great plan, and after having prioritized the various tasks to fulfill the plan, it will be necessary to do the third task: Perform. You must act. Every goal requires action. In fact, a goal without action is merely a wish. Many people wish, but few people perform. Success is the difference between wishing and performing.

If you want to have financial success the exact same principles apply. You must first plan, you must then prioritize the steps needed to achieve the plan, and then finally, you must perform. You must act. You must execute your plan. No house was ever built without action. Planning and prioritizing will yield nothing if you do not perform. Failure to complete all 3 Ps, and in the correct order, will inevitably lead to failure. Successful completion of all 3 Ps, and in the correct order, will inevitably lead to success.

Did you notice that the 3 Ps of success are effectively the same steps as the three steps to gaining financial wisdom discussed in the previous chapter? Planning equates to knowledge; Prioritising equates to consequences; Performing equates to action.

I want to share with you a story that I heard long ago. The story is of an old farmer who needed to hire a farm hand to help him out. The old farmer had a difficult time getting applicants for the job. Finally, a young man applied. When asked what his credentials were, the young man simply replied, "I can sleep when the wind blows." The old farmer thought that was a peculiar answer, but not having any other options he decided to hire the young man. One night, several months later, a tremendous storm blew in. The old farmer awoke frantically and rushed to alert the young man to get the farm ready to withstand the vicious storm that was fast approaching. To his dismay, he could not wake up the young man. Desperate to get everything prepared for the storm, he rushed out into the wind to take care of everything himself. He first went to the chickens but found that all the chickens were already safely secured inside the chicken coop. He then went to the haystack and saw that it was already secured and covered by a tarp. He ran to check on his cows and found that they were already safely in the barn. He checked the barn and discovered the shutters were all safely secured, and the doors securely barred. He soon realized there was nothing for him to do. It had all been done. The farm was ready for the storm. As he went back to his bed, he remembered that strange statement the young man had said months ago, "I can sleep when the wind blows." He now understood that strange statement.

Why can the young man sleep when the wind blows? Because he follows the 3 Ps.

Some of the steps may have been quick to perform, but he did follow them. First, he planned what would need to be done if a major storm blew in. He then determined which steps needed to be done and when. In other words, he prioritized. Finally, he acted. He performed. He did all the necessary steps before he went to bed. He followed the 3 Ps and in the correct order. Because he did that, he was able to sleep when the wind blew.

If you follow the financial 3 Ps in this book, you too will be able to sleep when the financial wind blows.

KEY TAKEAWAY:
    1. Success is a product of the 3 Ps. Plan, Prioritize, Perform.
    1. Success is the difference between wishing and performing.

PART II

CREATING THE PLAN

CREATING THE MAN

5

PLAN YOUR FINANCIAL FUTURE

Now that you know the 3 Ps of success, let's apply them to your personal finances. If you want to be financially successful, the first thing you need to do is plan. You need to set your financial goals. In setting those goals you need to think about today and tomorrow. You need to think about what you want your future to look like. Ask yourself, Where do I see myself in 30 years? In 20 years? In 10 years? In 1 year? Be precise but also be flexible. You cannot just say, in 20 years I will be living the good life, or in 20 years I will be travelling the world. That is not precise enough.

How do you define the "good life," and do you know what your expenses will be to enjoy that good life? Is the good life living in New York City, eating fancy dinners and going to Broadway shows and museums? Or is the good life living in a quiet cabin in the woods? If you are going to "travel the world," does that mean you are going to permanently live on a cruise ship or simply go on various tours once a year? You must ask yourself, What is my desired lifestyle, and what income is needed to achieve that desired lifestyle? How much will each option cost? Every good goal needs to be measurable and timely, i.e., in 20 years, I will have x dollars in the bank, or I will have y dollars of passive income. (Passive income is income that you receive without having to work, such as pensions, dividends, interest, and royalties.)

Early in my career, I determined that by the time I was age 55, I wanted to have five different sources of passive income, each one generating a minimum of $50,000. I had a specific number in mind and a specific time frame in which to achieve it. This goal created many subgoals and drove many of my decisions thereafter. This specific thinking is all part of the planning.

As you think your plan through, understand that there are trade-offs to be made. There is often a trade-off between leisure time and money. One is not necessarily better than the other. Both are needed, but you need to choose how much of each one you want to have. You must prioritize. You must understand that the decisions you make today will undoubtedly impact your life tomorrow. If you spend every penny that you make today, you will not have any money for tomorrow. If you do not spend any money today, you may have money for tomorrow, but you may not like your quality of life today. Thus, what is the correct balance? What do you choose? There is no right or wrong answer. Each person will make a different decision and that is okay, provided you understand, and accept, the consequences of your decisions.

As you make your plan, you need to remember that your decisions today impact your tomorrow. Find the balance between today and tomorrow. I recall a young couple that got married while they were both still in school. Shortly after they got married, they furnished their apartment with furniture, TVs, and "toys" that their parents had. They quickly spent all the money they received as wedding presents and then used up their credit cards. They soon had all the toys they needed to enjoy life while going to school.

As I watched that unfold, I questioned the wisdom of those decisions and of how that would impact them in the future. I felt like I was helplessly watching an impending train wreck. Sure enough, they quickly realized the decisions they'd made only a short time ago were financially foolish. Bills came in, credit card payments became due, and no cash was available. I remember talking to the wife shortly after all these purchases. She was weeping as she realized the short-term financial decisions of the past were now haunting their present. The train had crashed.

They had failed to plan. They had failed to realize that the outcome of tomorrow is a result of the decisions made today. They did not complete the first P, and they paid a painful price. Learn from their example. Avoid the train crash. Make sure to plan.

KEY TAKEAWAYS:
   Plan your future. Ask yourself the following:
      1. Where do I see myself in 1 year, 10 years, 20 years, and 30 years?
      2. What steps do I have to take to get there?
      3. Am I happy with the life balance I will create when I take those steps?

6

OWN YOUR MISTAKES

Financial success also requires being precise and being flexible. If your plan is executed flawlessly, you are lucky. There will always be setbacks, but if you are constantly facing setbacks, perhaps your plan is flawed. That is why every good plan needs to be flexible. You do not know what the future holds, and you do not know what challenges you will face. Thus, you must be flexible. You must be able to react to unforeseen obstacles that will undoubtedly come your way.

Earlier I mentioned that my plan was to create five different sources of income, each earning at least $50,000 in passive income. I remember when I had achieved my first pool of passive income. I had made an investment in a publicly traded company that paid regular dividends. The size of the investment was such that I would generate the $50,000 a year in dividends. I was proud of myself and felt good that my first pool had been created.

Unfortunately, I was not as financially wise as I thought. I had put too much of my investment into one stock. For reasons beyond my control, I had to sell that stock and at a loss. I soon realized that I had made a mistake by putting too much of my investment portfolio into one stock. I had taken on too much risk by putting too many eggs in one basket. If I wanted security, I needed to change my plan, and I needed to change it quickly.

In other words, I needed to be flexible. My plan A had not worked out the way I had envisioned. So, I learned and adapted. My plan B worked much better.

If I had not adjusted, my mistake would have just compounded, and things would have gotten worse. If you realize you made a mistake, be flexible, admit your mistake, and adjust right away. You are much better off to experience a small amount of pain today than a large amount of pain tomorrow. No road to success is a straight line, but you should do everything you can to keep the downturns as small as possible. You do this by being flexible. If you make a mistake, admit it early and correct it. Be flexible with your plan. No plan will be perfect.

Key Takeaways:
    1. Be flexible.
    2. Own your mistakes.

7

PLAN FOR THE WORST, HOPE FOR THE BEST

Sometimes life gets in the way of the best-laid plans. There are many circumstances beyond our control that can get in the way. Some we can plan for, others we cannot, but we must always plan for the worst. We must always assume that anything than can go wrong will go wrong, and then we build a plan to account for that. Let me give you a couple of specific examples.

Today, almost everyone owns a car. They buy the car to give them mobility, as well as the ability to travel, shop, and even get to work. However, what happens if you are in an accident and the car gets ruined and needs repairs? How do you manage that expense? The answer is obvious: car insurance. I think pretty much everybody who buys car insurance is hoping that they never need it. They grumble at the expense of insurance, but if they ever need to file a claim, they are grateful that they have insurance. Hoping for the best is buying a car and enjoying it for whatever purpose you bought it. Planning for the worst is buying insurance in case you have an accident and have expenses you cannot afford to pay.

Another example is life insurance. People who buy life insurance do not need it for themselves. They are dead. They buy life insurance to make sure those that they love are taken care of when they are gone. When I was newly married and still in school, with two small children, I bought life insurance. I hoped I would never need it; I planned my life on the belief I would never need it. I hoped for the best, but I also knew that life throws curveballs. I knew I could not predict the future and that even though statistically I had a small chance of dying, the chance was not zero. Therefore, I needed to do something to provide for my family in case I died. I needed to plan for the worst. The answer was life insurance. This gave both me and my wife some peace of mind. It reduced stress knowing that if I died, my family would at least have a little support to get their lives going and to move on.

Here is another example that does not involve insurance. When I was growing up, my dad started up and ran a highly successful real estate brokerage company. In fact, he became one of the largest and most successful independent brokerage companies in our area. It provided my family with the above-average comforts of life. One day, a large national company came by and offered to buy my dad's business, and he decided to sell. Years after he sold, I asked him why he sold. I will never forget his answer; it taught me a lot. He said he sold to make sure that my mom was taken care of in case anything happened to him. Here is a man who hoped for the best but planned for the worst. One of his biggest fears, if not his biggest fear, was that his wife would not be provided for after he died. So, he planned for the worst and sold his business to try and make sure the worst never happened.

As a side note, after my dad died, we learned that he had kept a life insurance policy on himself for decades. Even when times were extremely difficult, and they had no money, he kept his life insurance premiums current. He was always planning for the worst and planning to make sure his wife was always taken care of.

Hope for the best, but plan for the worst. It will reduce the stress in your life knowing that you have a plan in place if the worst happens.

Another example of planning for the worst but hoping for the best is writing a will. We all know that we will die one day. We all hope for that day to be sometime in the future, yet sadly, for many people it comes sooner than they would like. We can and should plan and hope for a long and happy life, but we must also be realistic and understand that not everyone is granted that luxury. To plan for the worst, we need a will. A will ensures that your assets are distributed in accordance with what you want, as opposed to what the government wants. If you die with a will, the will becomes a legal document that determines the handling of your estate. If you do not have a will, there is no document detailing your wishes, so your estate is handled based on the government's wishes. For instances where there is no will, the government has generally passed laws such that the government decides how your assets are transferred. You might think all your assets are automatically transferred to your spouse, but that is not necessarily the case. The government may have other plans. The only way to ensure your desires are fulfilled is to have a will. Hope for the best, but plan for the worst. Get a will.

Here's one last example about planning for the worst but hoping for the best. Years ago, I had a client come to see me for financial advice. Her husband, a senior executive for a major publicly traded corporation, had died unexpectedly, leaving her a middle-aged widow with little, if any, experience in finance. She was left to settle the estate, arrange for all the required government filings, including taxes, and try and put her own financial life in order. Her husband had handled all the finances. She did not know what assets they had, nor did she know where to look or how to find out. I gave her some guidance and agreed to meet with her the next week when she had a bit more information. When I saw her the second time she literally broke down and sobbed in my office. The whole situation was overwhelming. My heart broke for her. I did the best I could to help, but the reality was there was little I could do. As she sobbed in my office, I quietly vowed to myself that I would never let that happen to my wife. Make sure both spouses are fully informed about each other's financial affairs. If you die unexpectedly, the surviving spouse will be forced to deal with everything, and they need to at least know where to start.

In my case, I keep a personal financial statement, which I update at least annually. I list out all our assets and liabilities. I list out the estimated value. I also list out a contact person for each investment. I have gone over it with my wife, and she knows exactly where to find a copy. If I were to suddenly die, I know that she will have all the information she will need to continue to financially manage. I hope that day never happens. I hope for the best, but I have planned for the worst. Keep your partner informed and educated on all your finances.

Key Takeaways:
1. **Plan for the worst, hope for the best.**
2. **Have a will.**
3. **Keep your spouse fully informed on all family finances.**

PART III

PRIORITIZING THE PLAN

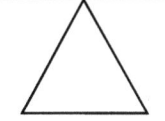

RECREATING THE MAN

8

A FOUR-LETTER WORD FOR FREEDOM

Now you have a good sense for the importance of planning. You realize that you will not achieve your financial goals without sitting down and making a plan. Let's assume you have even determined all the tasks you need to complete to achieve your plan. Now what? Well, the first thing you need to do is prioritize the action items that you said you would take. Do not try to put the roof on the building before you have built your foundation and your walls. I know that sounds obvious, but you would be surprised at how many people do that financially.

Early in my career, I got convinced by some smooth-talking salesperson to invest in copper options. This was a mistake. I did not understand the copper market; I did not understand options; I did not understand the futures market. I did not understand anything. Nonetheless, I went ahead and invested. I lost 100% of that investment. Why did I lose it? Because I tried to put the roof on before I had walls. I had not prioritized. I did not understand that a prerequisite to a smart decision (investment) is an informed decision (investment). Since I had failed to fulfill the prerequisite to a smart decision, my decision was destined to fail. I might have gotten lucky and made a profit, but that would have been pure luck. In hindsight, I am not sure it would have been a good thing if the decision (investment) had paid off because I would not have been educated by my mistake, and then I probably would have made an even bigger, more expensive mistake in the future.

I am grateful I was smart enough to only invest a small amount, so my education was relatively cheap. However, if I had understood the concept of prioritizing steps, and if I had made sure I was informed before I invested, I could have avoided the loss entirely.

What can the average person learn from my mistake? They can learn that when it comes to financial decisions (all decisions really), they must first inform themselves, and then, based on that information, make the decision that is best for them. The better the information, the better the decision.

In the area of personal finance, the best way to inform ourselves and gain the necessary information is to build a budget. The budgeting process will give us all the information we need to make informed decisions. It will inform us of our true cash inflows and our true cash outflows—meaning how our income is actually spent, not how we think it is spent. A budget will give us knowledge, and with that knowledge, we will have the power to make better decisions.

I know that to many the word "budget" sounds like a four-letter word. It is not. It is the key to information. The key to becoming informed. It is another word for freedom. A budget is the one way that everyone can take financial control of their lives. Creating a budget is what gives you the knowledge to help you set your financial priorities. It is what allows you to take control over your finances. It is what empowers you. You need to be informed; you need to build a budget.

However, before you build a budget, you need to understand a little bit about what a budget is and what a budget is not. We will discuss this in the following chapter.

Key Takeaways:
   1. **The prerequisite to a smart decision is an informed decision.**
   2. **The better the information, the better the decision.**
   3. **Creating a budget creates informed decisions.**
   4. **Creating a budget must be a priority.**

9

THE IS AND THE IS NOT

Budgeting is an interesting concept. It is poorly understood and often poorly implemented. In fact, budgeting is the foundation of all sound financial management, not just personal financial management. I doubt there is a successful business in the world that does not have a solid and robust budgeting process.

There are only two kinds of people in this world who don't need to budget—those who have so few wants that they are happy with nothing, and those who have so much money that their money will always exceed their wants. (Perhaps like a Bill Gates or a Warren Buffett.) If you are not one of those two types, then you need to budget; and if you are going to budget, then you need to understand what budgeting *is* and what budgeting *is not*.

Let's start with what budgeting *is not* and clear up a few misconceptions of budgeting.

1. Budgeting **is not** a four-letter word.
2. Budgeting **is not** about losing control of one's finances.
3. Budgeting **is not** about math.
4. Budgeting **is not** about money. (Perhaps the most surprising one of all.)

Now then, having mentioned what budgeting *is not*, let's talk about what budgeting *is*.

1. Budgeting **is** about freedom.
2. Budgeting **is** about taking control.

3. Budgeting **is** about *you* deciding.
4. Budgeting **is** about prioritizing. (There is that P word again.)
5. Budgeting **is** about acquiring wealth.
6. Budgeting **is** about controlling your emotions.

People are often afraid to budget because they are afraid they will lose their freedom. In fact, just the opposite is true. Budgeting is what creates freedom. People want the ability to decide what to spend and when to spend it, and they seem to think that budgeting will take this away. Nothing could be further from the truth. In fact, it is only through the budgeting process that they can truly gain control over spending decisions, i.e., what to spend and when to spend.

If we are not truly the master of spending decisions, then we have lost control of our finances. Worse yet, we have voluntarily given up control. We have lost our financial freedom. Budgeting is about taking back our financial freedom. It is about *taking* control instead of *being* controlled. It is the key to gaining financial freedom.

A proper budget allows you to understand your cash inflows and your cash outflows. It allows you to then match your outflows to your inflows and make sure your outflows do not exceed your inflows. When your cash inflows exceed your cash outflows, even by only one dollar, you have put yourself on the road to financial freedom. However, if your cash outflows exceed your cash inflows, even by one dollar, you have put yourself on the road to financial stress and misery. These laws are irrefutable. You cannot break them; you can only break yourself against them.

Proper budgeting puts you in control of your finances. It allows you to decide where you want to spend your money. It allows you to allocate your money to where it will benefit you the most. If you are worried about future expenses, such as retirement, education, or even simple vacations, budgeting allows you to provide for these things. In short, budgeting allows you to take financial control, as opposed to being controlled. It frees you from financial stresses. It liberates you. Who would not want all that?

Part of taking control of your finances is allowing yourself to decide, in advance, how you want to spend your money. It eliminates the impulse purchases and allows you to direct your funds to where they will do you the most good. When it comes to finances and control, there are only two options. Either you control your finances, or your finances control you. Whether you control your finances, or your finances control you is entirely up to you—but make no mistake, there will be control. If you budget, you will be in control; if you do not budget, your finances will be in control. It is that simple. Do you want to control or be controlled?

Choosing to be controlled is the road to financial stress and misery. Choosing to control is the road to financial freedom and happiness. These laws are irrefutable and cannot be broken. The choice is yours, and while you are free to make any choice you want, you are not free from the consequences of your choices. So, choose wisely. And make sure the consequences of your choices are the consequences you desire.

Budgeting allows you to prioritize your expenditures so that you are spending your money where you want to spend it. No one tells you how or where to spend your money. Only you do that. But a proper budget will allow you to decide where your money goes so that your personal objectives are met. You do this by prioritizing where your money is spent. That way, you know that each dollar is going where it provides you the most benefit.

I am constantly amazed at people who spend money on fast food and takeout dinners only to get to the end of the month and not have enough money for their rent or mortgage payment. They clearly have not prioritized their spending, but they do it time and time again. They have chosen to be controlled and not to control.

There is an adage: "What is the first thing you should do when you find yourself in a hole? Quit digging." If you find yourself in a financial hole, you need to quit digging. Budgeting allows you to not only quit digging, but also to start filling the hole. It is only by becoming the master of your finances that you will be able to build up your resources and start acquiring wealth. If you do not budget, you will not become the master of your resources, and you will not acquire wealth. Thus, budgeting is the first key to acquiring wealth.

Finally, budgeting is about controlling your emotions. Too often people impulse buy. They spend their money on the spur of the moment because they are feeling pressured or because it makes them feel good or because it makes them look good. These are decisions based on emotions, and they are often stressful decisions. It is an internal battle every time.

However, if you prepare a budget and prepare it when you are not feeling pressured, two good things happen. First, you make a spending decision without emotion and based on what is in your best personal interest. Second, you only make the decision once. When you are tempted to buy something, or when you are feeling pressured to buy something, you do not have to agonize over it time and time again. You have already made the decision, and you know it was the right decision. Making the same decision repeatedly is stressful. Making it once and then moving on with your life is stress-free. Thus, budgeting allows you to take control of your emotions and thereby reduce the stress in your life.

Key Takeaways:
1. **Creating a budget must be a priority.**
2. **Budgeting allows you to take control of your finances, as opposed to having your finances control you.**
3. **When you find yourself in a financial hole, quit digging.**
4. **Budgeting allows you to take control of your emotions and thereby reduce the stress in your life.**
5. **You are free to make any choices you want, but you are not free from the consequences of your choices.**

10

BUY THE MILK FIRST

Budgeting is a great freedom fighter. It is by far the best weapon available to create financial freedom. The question therefore becomes: Why is budgeting such a great freedom fighter? What happens in the budgeting process that suddenly allows me to be free? The answer can be given in one word: priorities.

When my parents were newly married, they were very poor. Although they were blessed with a baby girl, they had no money. My dad was going to school full time during the day, and he worked as a custodian at night. They were always worried that their money would run out before the month did. Therefore, they had to learn how to budget. They had to apply the rules of prioritization.

So, at the end of each month, when my dad got paid, my parents had two priorities. First, they paid the rent for the next month. Second, they went out and bought enough milk for my sister to make sure she had enough food for the month. If they were going to run out of food, my mom and dad figured they would go hungry, but they were never going to let their baby girl go hungry. Although they had lots of expenses (including food for themselves), they understood the rules of prioritization. Their highest priority was their daughter, and they made sure that their limited money went first to providing a roof over her head and second to buying food for her to eat. All other expenses were a lower priority. There were months when the money did run out before the month did, but their baby girl never suffered.

We all have a long list of activities we would like to do or items we would like to acquire. We also have limited resources and therefore lack the ability to do or acquire all the things on our list. How then do we best resolve this dilemma? How do we decide where to apply our limited resources? We solve this problem by applying the two simple rules of prioritization.

The two rules of prioritization are remarkably simple, yet it is surprising how many people fail to follow the rules. They are:

1. Prioritize your list of wants and needs.
2. Never let a lower priority take precedence over a higher priority. Never.

If you can follow these two simple rules, your life will be much more fulfilling. Those who apply these two simple rules to their personal finances will be successful in their personal finances. Further, those who apply these two simple rules in life will be successful in life. The rules of prioritization cross boundaries and apply to all aspects of life, not just personal finances. The more that one applies these rules, the more successful one will be. It is that simple. If my parents had not learned how to budget and if they had not understood the rules of prioritization, their daughter would have suffered and gone hungry—but she never did. That creates freedom from stress and freedom from worry. I am sure they felt a lot of financial stress in the early years of their marriage, but they did not stress about how they would feed their daughter. That was their top priority, and it was always taken care of. I am confident that when finances looked tight, they took comfort in knowing that their daughter was taken care of. They prioritized what was most important, and they never let a lower priority take precedence over a higher priority.

Even though this sounds easy, simple, and logical, there are many who do not do this and therefore add unnecessary stress to their life. Reduce the stress, prioritize, and then respect the priorities. The lesson we should all learn from this is simple. Figure out your priorities; then always address your highest priority first. In other words, buy the milk first. Your life will be better if you do.

Key Takeaways:
1. **Prioritize your list of wants and needs.**
2. **Never, never, never let a lower priority take precedence over a higher priority. Never.**

11

THE RULE OF FINANCIAL HAPPINESS

There is not necessarily a right way or a wrong way to prepare your budget, but every budget should follow certain principles.

Prepare a Personal Income Statement
The first step in budgeting is proper preparation. As mentioned before, budgeting is just another word for prioritizing and planning. You are prioritizing your expenses, and then based on those priorities you are planning where you want to spend your money. However, before you plan for tomorrow, it is important to know where you are today. You need to be informed. To do that, you need to create a personal income statement.

A personal income statement is like a business income statement, it will tell you on one page exactly what your income and your expenses are.

I suggest your personal income statement cover an entire year. (One month is just too short a time and will not give you an accurate picture of all your expenses.) By looking back on the previous year, you will get a much more accurate picture of your financial situation. With a more accurate picture, you will be able to make better decisions. Your 12-month personal income statement will tell you, at a glance, where your money currently comes from and where it is currently going. Once you know that, you can decide where you want your money to go and adjust your spending accordingly. If you are like most people, you will be quite surprised when you learn where your income actually goes.

To prepare your personal income statement, you need to make sure that you have available all the relevant information concerning your current financial situation. If you are not an accountant this might sound like an ominous task, but it really is not. It is as simple as writing down where you get your cash from and where you are spending that cash. You then organize that information into categories.

Organizing the information into categories makes it easier for you to understand everything. In the old days, this would involve a lot of paper-pushing and gathering receipts. Nowadays, with electronic banking, it is much easier. Most banks now allow you to download all your transactions into a spreadsheet. So, to gather the information you need, go online and download all your banking transactions into a spreadsheet. Do this for each of your bank accounts, as well as your credit cards.

Then sort each file by description and create a subtotal for each different description. To do this, identify all the categories. Then place each description under a category.

For example, you might have several entries for "McDonald's." This would be each time you went to McDonald's. You can place the description "McDonald's" under the category "Fast Food" or "Eating Out." You might also have several line items with the description "Wendy's" or "Subway." Each of these descriptions would also fall under the category "Fast Food" or "Eating Out." You could then total up all the entries for "Fast Food" or "Eating Out," and you will know exactly how much money you spent on that category during the year.

Do this for each description—both your income and your expenses—until you have categorized each grouping of descriptions. Once every line item has been summarized and categorized, you are ready to create your own personal income statement.

Determine your income
I would suggest starting with income, as it is generally much easier and makes you feel good about getting one step done. Income is another word for sources of cash. If you are going to budget, you must know your sources of cash and how much cash each source generates. Go through all your categories of income that you identified in the above step and write them down

on your personal income statement. For most people, this will simply be their salary.

However, for many others it is more complicated. It could include interest payments, rental income, royalty payments, as well as dividends from investments, pension, or other annuities. Perhaps you do odd jobs and handyman work, or perhaps you do some babysitting. The key is to write down all your sources of cash. Remember you are creating a personal income statement for a one-year period, so be sure and capture all the income you earn in one year. Once you have properly identified your income, you are ready to move on to the next step.

Determine where you have spent your cash

The expense side is just like the income side, except it will require more categories. Go through all your categories of expenses (such as the "Fast Food" or "Eating Out" category I mentioned earlier) and write them down on your personal income statement. If you have a lot of cash expenses, you will need to assign it the best you can to one of your categories. If you are not sure, just create a category called "Cash Expenses." Over time, you will want to keep this category as close to nil as possible, but when you first start out, that may not be possible.

Additionally, some of your summarized items will apply to different categories on your budget. For example, Walmart expenses may fall under several categories, such as food, clothing, presents, or even a car. If you find yourself in this situation, you will need to go through your receipts to figure out how much should be assigned to each category. If you do not still have your receipts then: 1) give your best estimate as to how much Walmart expenses should be assigned to each category and 2) start keeping your receipts so you can record accurate information in the future.

Once you have copied all your expenses onto your personal income statement, you will be able to see, at a glance, where you have spent your money. If you are like most people, one or both of the following will happen: 1) you will be surprised at *how much* money you spent that you don't know where it went and 2) you will be surprised by *where* you actually spent your money, as opposed to where you originally thought you spent your money.

If either one of those scenarios describes you, it underscores the critical importance of completing these steps. Both of those situations are big financial stress creators. However, now that you have identified them, you are much better equipped to not only manage them but to conquer them.

Allocate your expenses between "fixed" expenses and "variable" expenses
Now that we have investigated the past, we are ready to start planning the future. The first step is to allocate your expenses between "fixed" (non-controllable expenses) and "variable" (controllable expenses). This is quite a simple step, yet it makes the planning process much easier. (Note: I call it "planning" because that is all that budgeting really is. It is the planning of expenses.)

Fixed expenses are those expenses that stay the same every month.

Fixed expenses represent those items for which we have already made a commitment to spend. Examples of these would be mortgage or rent payments, along with car payments and loan payments. If you have child support or alimony payments, those would also belong in this category. Another example would be insurance. Whether you pay this monthly or annually is irrelevant. What is relevant is that it is a fixed amount that you have already committed to.

A fixed expense is money that we have effectively already spent, even before we earned it. In other words, fixed expenses are expenses that you no longer control. Thus, another word for fixed expenses would be "non-controllable" expenses.

Many of our fixed expenses are not paid monthly. Rather they are paid annually or semi-annually. In these situations, take the amount of the payment and divide it by the number of months it covers. For example, if you pay insurance once a year, take your total insurance premium and divide it by 12. This will give you the monthly amount of insurance you pay. Put this number in your monthly budget for insurance. Even though you do not pay it monthly, you need to allow for it. Otherwise, you will spend your money each month, and then when the expenses that are paid annually are due, you will not have the funds to make the payment. This creates stress.

Variable expenses are those expenses that vary each month, or those expenses for which no prior fixed commitment has been made

Examples of variable expenses would be gas for the car, repairs to the car, groceries, entertainment (dinners, movies, and vacations), etc. In effect, these are the expenses that vary each month. Utilities could be either variable or fixed. If you are on a utility plan where you have committed to pay the same amount each month (like cable or internet subscriptions), it is a fixed expense. If the amount can vary, it is variable. In other words, variable expenses are expenses that you do control. Thus, another word for variable expenses would be "controllable" expenses. That is to say, those expenses for which no commitment has yet been made and that therefore you still have some control over that expense.

Now that you have identified your income, your fixed expenses, and your variable expenses, you are ready for the final step in creating your personal income statement. This is, by far, the simplest step of them all and is accomplished by completing the following tasks:

1. Put all your income items at the top of your income statement, with a subtotal for "Total Income."
2. Create a heading labelled "Fixed Expenses" and list all the fixed expenses that you have identified.
3. Create a subtotal for "Fixed Expenses."
4. Create a line labelled "Available Cash after Fixed Expenses" and put that under your subtotal for fixed expenses. On that line, enter the amount you get by subtracting your subtotal "Fixed Expenses" from your "Total Income." This is an important line because this is the amount that you really have left to budget.
5. Create another heading, "Variable Expenses," and list the variable expenses that you have identified.
6. Create a subtotal for "Variable Expenses."
7. Create a line labelled "Excess/Deficit Cash Available."
8. Subtract the subtotal for "Variable Expenses" from the "Available Cash after Fixed Expenses."

Congratulations! You have now created your personal income statement. And you have now identified either the amount of cash you have left over or the amount of cash you are short. You are now ready to start building your budget and eliminating the financial stresses in your life.

Your personal annual income statement should look something like the following.

INCOME

Salary (Net Take-Home Pay)	$50,000.00
Rent	2,500.00
Interest	500.00
Total Income	$53,000.00

EXPENSES

Fixed Expenses

Tithes/Charitable Giving	$5,300.00
Savings	6,000.00
Rent/Mortgage	15,000.00
Car Payment	6,000.00
Cable/Internet	1,200.00
Investing	2,000.00
Subtotal Fixed Expenses	$35,500.00
Available Cash after Fixed Expenses	$17,500.00

Variable Expenses

Fuel	$600.00
Groceries	12,000.00
Presents	1,000.00
Clothing	2,000.00
Entertainment	900.00
Utilities	6,000.00
Subtotal Variable Expenses	$22,500.00
Excess/(Deficit) Cash Available	$(5,000.00)

Buy the Milk First

Now that you have identified your income and determined where your money has been going, you can sit down and decide where your money *should* be going. Up until now, your money may have been controlling you. This is where you can now take control of your money.

Ask yourself, Is this spending pattern going to achieve my previously set goals and ambitions? Will this allow me to get to where I want to be in 1 year, 10 years, 20 years, or 30 years from now? If you are one of the rare people who can answer yes, congratulations! Now ask yourself, Can I make some changes to help me get there faster? If you are like most people and answer no, you need to ask yourself, What changes can I make in my spending to help me achieve my plan?

In my oversimplified example, you will note two key points. First, there is a line item for "Savings," which is included under "Fixed Expenses." Second, this person is currently running a deficit, meaning they are spending more money than they are making.

Regarding the line item for "Savings," it is not a coincidence that savings is under "Fixed expenses." Nor is it a coincidence that "Savings" is second only to "Tithes/Charitable Giving" on the list. That is because I believe you should pay your tithes first and yourself second. (A tithe is one tenth, or ten percent, of your income, given to your church.)

Then paying yourself second, and ahead of all other expenses, is important. It is what creates your investment and savings account. It is what allows you to plan for the future, and last but certainly not least, it forces you to live within your means. If you do not live within your means, you will forever be in financial bondage to others. You will never achieve your financial goals, and your life will be full of unnecessary and painful financial stress.

This brings us to the second key point to note: this person is running a deficit. This is a sure road to misery. It is a violation of the Rule of Financial Happiness and a violation of the Rule of Financial Happiness will always result in misery. The Rule of Financial Happiness is amazingly simple and can be written as a mathematical equation.

$$\text{Cash Inflow} > \text{Cash Outflow} = \text{Financial Happiness}$$

$$\text{Cash Inflow} < \text{Cash Outflow} = \text{Stress and Misery}$$

These formulas are true even if the difference is only one dollar. The individual in this example is a sinking ship. They are taking on debt through a higher mortgage, lines of credit, or credit cards—all of which are bad. All of which puts the individual in financial bondage and results in stress and misery. The next two chapters will discuss how to avoid this situation and what to do if you are already in this situation.

However, before we move on, there is one more critical comment to make. If you do all the above, but fail to stay on top of it, if you fail to continually monitor your spending, it will avail you nothing. You must take the above steps and then monitor yourself to make sure your actual spending is consistent with your desired spending (your budget). You can do the monitoring manually or you can use some of the various software services available to make this task easier. Three of the better apps that can help you do all this are Simplifi, Mvelopes or YNAB (you need a budget). Each has pros and cons, but they will all help you become a master of the above principles. I recommend you look at each of them (or others) and pick the one that works best for you.

Key Takeaways:
    Live by the Rule of Financial Happiness:
        1. Establish your fiscal priorities.
        2. Determine your cash inflows.
        3. Determine your cash outflows.
        4. Adjust your cash inflows and outflows such that . . .
            a. Cash inflows are greater than cash outflows.
            b. Cash outflows match your priorities.

12

DOING WHAT YOU WANT WITH WHAT YOU GOT

Now that you know where your money was spent, and you have determined where you would like to be financially in the future, the next step is to decide how to spend your money to align your spending today with achieving your vision for tomorrow. This is why we divided our expenses into "Fixed Expenses" and "Variable Expenses."

Using the example in the prior chapter, you might think that since your total annual income is $53,000, you have $53,000 to budget, but you do not. You only have $17,500 to budget. That is because your fixed expenses have already been determined. Remember, you do not control these expenses. The day you took on a car payment, you already decided to spend money on car payments and agreed to relinquish control over to this expense. Thus, it needs to come out of your budget.

Now go through each line item under your "Variable Expenses" and ask yourself the following:

1. Is this an expense I need to make?
2. Does it need to be a higher amount? A lower amount?
3. Is this expense taking away funds from a higher priority?

This last question is critical. In fact, it should be asked every time. The whole purpose of the budgeting process is to make sure that your money is being spent where you most want it spent. Asking this question regularly is a great way to make sure that money is being spent on your highest priorities and that therefore you are achieving your goals. However, there is one other step that is critical in making sure that your budget aligns with your goals.

Two of the most common long-term goals are: 1) provide for retirement and 2) provide for a child's future education. Both objectives require putting funds away for the future. If you look at the simplified budget in the previous chapter, you will note two items under "Fixed Expenses"—one for "Savings" and one for "Investments."

Savings is intended to be a short-term emergency fund. For example, your car breaks down and it needs repairs, or a major appliance broke and you need a new one. These are not in your regular budget, but they are something that needs to be planned for and budgeted for. You can do this by building up a "short-term emergency fund" that you can draw on for these one-time, irregular expenses.

Once you have a sufficient short-term emergency fund built up, you can allocate these funds to a different category, such as "Investments." The investment account is different from the savings account in that it is meant to be funds for long-term needs, such as retirement or college.

As you start out, the size of the savings account or the investment account is not as relevant as simply having one. Even if you only put one dollar into each, that is a start. Then you can grow it as circumstances change. The key point is to have these accounts and to have them as fixed expenses. Why is this important? Because it is the driver of another unbreakable financial law: Pay yourself first.

When you build your budget, you need to pay yourself first. This forces you to follow the Rule of Financial Happiness. It is a key step in making sure that you are not surviving by taking on debt. Additionally, it ensures your budget aligns with your priorities. If your priority is being able to retire or fund a college education for a child, but you never set funds aside to make that happen, then you are letting a lower priority (a more short-term) expense take precedence over a higher priority. This breaks a fundamental financial law and will never lead to any good. At this point, some people may say that this all makes sense, but the reality is they just do not have the money to make this happen. That brings us to our next chapter.

Buy the Milk First

Key Takeaways:
1. Build a budget that aligns with your goals.
2. Pay yourself first.
3. Put money into a short-term emergency fund.
4. Put money into a long-term investment fund.

13

HELP! I AM SHORT OF FUNDS

You will note that in the sample budget from Chapter 11, that person was running a deficit, meaning their cash outflows exceeded their cash inflows. This is never a good thing and is a sure way to create financial pain and stress. Unfortunately, this is quite common. People generally find themselves in this situation because they have violated one particularly important financial law. Recall the second key takeaway in Chapter 10: **Never, never, never let a lower priority take precedence over a higher priority. Never.** People usually violate this law in one of two ways.

First, what happens is people give in to the impulse buy. They tell themselves, it is just an ice cream cone, or it is just lunch at McDonald's, or it is just a really cute pair of shoes that will go perfectly with my outfit. Whatever it is, if it was not originally in the budget, then it is a lower priority, and by making that purchase, you are taking funds away from something that you previously determined was a higher priority. Thus, you are now letting a lower priority take precedence over a higher priority, and you are breaking this especially important financial law. The consequence of breaking this law is that you are trading off short-term and temporary pleasure for long-term financial pain and stress. Reduce your stress. Do not break this law.

A second reason people find themselves in this situation is because a particular expense is in their budget that should not be. If you are running a deficit and your cash outflows exceed your cash inflows, your budget has too many expenses. You have put expenses in your budget that you cannot afford. In this scenario, the same financial law applies. **Never, never, never let a lower priority take precedence over a higher priority. Never.**

Now that we have clearly established that cash outflows exceeding cash inflows is a priorities problem, let's talk about three ways to fix this problem.

Some of these solutions may seem rather obvious, but they still need to be said.

1. Reduce Expenses.
2. Increase Income.
3. Change Lifestyle.

Reduce Expenses

If you find yourself in a deficit position, the first place to start fixing the problem is your variable expenses. What expenses can you eliminate? Note that I said, "Variable Expenses." These are the expenses that you have not already committed to and that are the easiest to change. Remember in the short-term, you do not control your fixed expenses. Those expenses have already been committed to. That is why you start with only looking at your controllable or variable expenses.

As you look over your variable expenses, ask yourself questions like, Do I need to eat out as often as I do? Can I change my diet? Can I get away with buying less expensive clothes or birthday presents or Christmas presents? Look at every line item and ask yourself, Do I really need this? Is there a less expensive option?

I was once asked to help a single mother who had a huge deficit in her budget and was relying on the charity of others to close the gap. So, I went through all the financial procedures outlined above, and I was shocked by what I discovered. For example, she had the most expensive cable package imaginable with many of the add-ons. Her cable package far exceeded my own, and I had more children and no financial problems. This is clearly an expense that could be eliminated. Making small changes such as these would free up funds to cover her higher priority expenses.

For my own personal life, I got married while still in university, and we had two children by the time I graduated, followed by our third child ten months after I graduated. We went through several periods where, in looking at our budget, it appeared we were going to run a deficit. Each time it happened, my wife and I agreed to go into what we affectionately called "cheap mode." We ate a lot of Kraft Dinner and Rice-A-Roni. And we found we could feed ourselves and our children for pennies. We did not buy new clothes; we just made do a little longer with whatever we had. For Christmas, we even bought all our children's presents from garage sales. They were young, they never knew, and they certainly did not care.

Eventually I would get a pay raise, and it would be enough to bring us out of "cheap mode." Then if things got tight again, we would just go back into "cheap mode." In effect, what we did was reduce expenses. We looked at all our line items on our personal income statement and decided which ones we could either temporarily do without or we could do with less of.

If you find yourself running a deficit, do what my wife and I did. Take a hard look at your expenses and figure out what you can do without. Many people will be surprised by how much they can reduce their expenses if they just give it a little thought, effort, and commitment.

Increase Income

Another option is to increase income. In my case, we were willing to go into "cheap mode" because we knew it was temporary. I had a good job that I knew would get annual pay increases. Thus, when I got my pay increase, I no longer needed to eliminate the deficit by cutting expenses—I could do it by increasing my income. I did this by getting pay raises, but you can also increase income by taking on another job. That is what my wife did to help us out.

As it turns out, my wife is very entrepreneurial with a strong business sense. To create extra income, she started a home-based dry goods gourmet food business. She chose this business because she noticed that whenever she went to craft shows, all the consumers were carrying bags with gourmet food. Over time, her small home business grew out of the home and into a warehouse, the business continued to grow and she eventually sold the business to focus on yet a different business, but the gourmet food business started out as a small side hustle just to earn more income. If you have cut your expenses the best you can, but you still have a deficit, look at increasing your income. Take on another job or start a small home business. Who knows, your home business might grow into something substantial. Many do.

Change Lifestyle

If you cannot eliminate the deficit by reducing expenses or increasing income (or you choose not to), there is still a third option. Go back to your expenses but now look at the fixed expenses. Truth be known, fixed expenses are only fixed for the short-term. You can change a fixed expense, but it requires that you change your lifestyle. You know that new car that you love to drive? Well, maybe you need to get rid of it and trade it in for a cheaper model. That could reduce or even eliminate your car payment. It will also save on insurance. Additionally, ask yourself questions like, Do I really need cable T.V? Can I downgrade my phone plan? Do I have subscriptions services that I do not really need? Those are all fixed expenses, but perhaps you can transfer to a less expensive option (or even eliminate the expense altogether).

If those options do not appeal to you, perhaps you need to move. Sell your home and buy a less expensive home with a smaller mortgage payment. If you are renting, move out and find another place to rent with lower rent. It may not be as nice a place to live, but if you have a deficit and have already looked at reducing variable expenses or increasing income, you are living beyond your means. These fixed expenses might feel good today, but if you are running a deficit, you are planting noxious weeds. I guarantee you that come harvest time, these excess expenses will lead to financial pain, stress, and outright misery. You must eliminate the deficit in your budget. No excuses.

Remember your priorities and keep them straight. If you are not prepared to do any of these three things, I am quite sure you have your priorities reversed, and you are letting a lower priority take precedence over a higher priority. Never do that. Never.

Key Takeaways:
   To balance your budget:
      1. Reduce Expenses.
      2. Increase Income.
      3. Change Lifestyle.

14

DEBT: THE GOOD, THE BAD, AND THE UGLY

You will never be able to create wealth if you do not know how to manage debt. Managing debt is a fundamental principle that must be mastered before wealth can be created. However, you cannot manage debt without first understanding debt. Let's talk a little bit about what debt is, and then we can talk about how to manage it.

Understanding Debt
Debt is a wonderful servant but a horrible master. What do I mean by that? Once you take on debt, you become the servant, and the debt becomes your master. Everything you do is now for the benefit of your creditor. You have voluntarily given up your financial freedom, put yourself in financial bondage, and willingly relinquished control. Your debt has become your master. But debt is not a kind or generous master. Debt is a vicious, persistent, and relentless master. Debt does not care about you or your well-being. Debt never sleeps. Debt never takes a vacation. Debt creates stress. Debt creates financial pain and worry. Debt destroys lives. Debt is not your friend, and yet when you incur debt, you are inviting debt to live with you 24/7.

Many years ago, one of my graduate accounting professors told me that the American Bar Association estimated 80% of all divorces could be attributed to money. In fact, the American Bar Association jokingly said that the marriage vow should be changed to, "Till debt do us part." When people are incurring debt, they are making a conscious decision to exchange what could be a benefit today for a liability tomorrow. People's inability to control emotions and passions today is what prevents them from creating wealth tomorrow. Debt gives you something of lesser value today by stealing something of much greater value tomorrow.

Alternatively, those who create wealth understand this about debt. They become the ones who offer the loan and therefore are on the other side of debt. They are the ones who are using debt as a servant and not as a taskmaster. They reap all the benefits of debt while those who borrow the money incur all the costs of debt. In summary, those who understand debt become the creditors while those who do not understand debt become the debtors.

Managing Debt

Managing debt is critical to building wealth and removing financial stress. I have read many articles and listened to many advisors who say that there is good debt and bad debt. They say that good debt is debt for assets like a house, a car, or an education, and that bad debt is everything else. I respectfully, but vehemently, disagree.

In my opinion, there are three types of debt:

1. Good Debt
2. Bad Debt
3. Ugly Debt

Good Debt

Good debt is the rarest of all forms of debt. Given how evil debt can be, it almost makes me cringe to even write the words "good debt." To me, good debt is almost an oxymoron. There is extraordinarily little debt that is good debt, but in rare instances, it is possible to have good debt.

Good debt must meet two conditions. First, it must be debt that is used to create wealth, i.e., it is never used for purchasing consumer products. Second, it must be debt that comes with absolutely no personal risk.

By no personal risk, I literally mean no personal risk. If you suddenly decide to quit making the debt payments, you are in no way, shape, or form liable for the debt. While this debt is rare, it does sometimes happen.

For example, let's say you found some real estate you want to buy. So, you form a corporation and use the corporation to buy the real estate. Then when you do buy the real estate, you arrange for the corporation to borrow the funds. Further, you make sure that there is no personal guarantee on the debt. (A guarantee is when the lender has the right to look to you for the debt payment, if the actual borrower—your corporation in this example—defaults on the debt.) In this situation, you have no personal liability. If your corporation quits making payments, the lender can take control of the real estate, but they cannot come to you for payments. Thus, if the value of the real estate goes up, you receive all the appreciation. If the value of the real estate goes down, you can quit making payments, and the lender gets the real estate. In this example, you get the upside potential but none of the downside risk (other than your initial investment).

However, banks and lenders are not stupid. They usually will not lend unless there is either a guarantee or a lot of equity protecting them against the downside scenario. Accordingly, this kind of debt is hard to come by. Sometimes a lender will try to "trick" you into a guarantee. They may use terms, such as "it is just a formality" or "it is just our bank's policy," implying that you do not really need to worry about it. If it is not that big a deal, then the banks do not need the guarantee.

I learned all this from my dad, after he endured a sad business experience. My dad once bought a business in the energy industry that he knew was going to be promising. In fact, his banker also thought it had such great promise that he quit his job to join my dad in the business. My dad signed a guarantee for the benefit of all the shareholders, not just himself. After all, it was "just a formality," he was told. Shortly after he bought the business, the government announced a major policy change and effectively nationalized the industry he was in. His contracts dried up overnight, and he was stuck with a worthless business and a bunch of bank debt. Suddenly the "formality" of the guarantee was no longer a formality. It was a binding legal agreement, and the bank expected payment. My dad made good on the debt, but he had to sell his house to do it.

I saw what that did to my dad, and I vowed I would never make the same mistake. And I never have. It has potentially cost me some upside in various business transactions, but it has also prevented a lot of downside. I have never regretted making this vow.

I previously mentioned my wife's dry gourmet food business. She ran that business through a corporation. However, the business was very cyclical. Most of the annual sales came in during a six-week period. She needed to build up her inventory throughout the year and then sell it all during that six-week period. I approached the bank about giving the corporation a line of credit to finance the inventory buildup. The bank was more than happy to oblige; they just needed my personal guarantee.

I looked my banker—who I had a good relationship with—in the eye and said, "I don't do guarantees. That is a deal-breaker for me."

He responded with, "It's a deal-breaker?"

I said, "Yes, it is a deal-breaker."

He said okay and still gave us the line of credit.

I was okay with this debt because: 1) it allowed us to create wealth through the business, and 2) there was no personal liability if something went wrong. Therefore, it met my definition of good debt.

Bad Debt

Bad debt is debt that comes with personal liability but is used to provide for basic needs. So even though it may be bad debt, it is still permissible debt, such as a mortgage. You need a place to live. You can rent, or you can buy. If you choose to buy, it is highly unlikely you will have the funds to pay cash. Thus, a mortgage becomes necessary. But just because it is necessary, and therefore permissible, does not mean it is good debt. It is still bad debt. Do not fool yourself into thinking otherwise.

Another example would be student loan debt. No student loan debt is good debt, but if it's debt that provides you with an education that will help increase your earning potential, it is permissible. Again, it is still bad debt, but it is permissible. However, never forget that these debts are still bad debts and that you should still get out of debt as soon as possible.

Ugly Debt

All other debt is ugly debt. This is the debt that is to be avoided at all costs. This is consumer debt: credit card debt. Debt incurred to pay for vacations or presents or entertainment. This is all ugly debt and should never be incurred. You must also be careful to not fool yourself into thinking that ugly debt is bad debt.

For example, I mentioned earlier that mortgage debt is bad debt. This is true, but if you are taking on a mortgage and payments that you cannot easily afford, then the bad debt becomes ugly debt. Likewise for student loan debt. Student loan debt can be bad debt, but it can also be ugly debt. If you are incurring student loan debt for a program that will not substantially increase your earning power, then you are incurring ugly debt.

I know some people personally, and I have read articles about others, who complain about their student loan debt. They went to university for four years, graduated with a degree, and now cannot get a job. When you dig deep into what degree they graduated with, it is often in a field with limited job opportunities. Although they took courses in a field that interested them, it is a field where they might struggle to increase their earning potential. If they choose to study in a field that has limited job prospects, that is okay. That is their decision and their right, but if they are incurring debt to finance that degree, they are violating a financial law which leads to negative outcomes. They need to understand that the debt they are incurring is ugly debt. It is certainly not good debt, and it is not bad debt. It is ugly debt and ugly debt should never be incurred, never. If they'd understood this simple debt principle at the beginning of their college education, they could have avoided the negative outcomes of breaking such a sacred financial law. They could have saved themselves a lot of money, a lot of financial pain, a lot of grief, and a lot of stress.

Ugly debt is always to be avoided. No exceptions. That is the law.

Use of Credit Cards
No discussion on debt is complete without a discussion on credit cards. First, let me say, credit cards are not necessarily bad. Credit cards are a two-edged sword. If used properly, they are beneficial. If used poorly, they are the worst kind of ugly debt. Unfortunately, too many people choose to use them poorly.

Four of the benefits of credit cards are:

1. Convenience
2. Record Keeping
3. Rewards
4. Online Purchases

Convenience

One of the benefits of a credit card is convenience. You do not need to carry cash. You take your credit card, you pay, and you go. You never have to worry, "Do I have enough cash with me to make this purchase?" However, debit cards provide the exact same convenience without the creation of ugly debt. So, if the only reason you are using credit cards is for convenience—Stop! Use debit cards instead. You will get all the benefits you are looking for without any of the drawbacks associated with ugly debt.

Record Keeping

Another benefit of a credit card is that it keeps a paper trail of your transactions. This way you always know what you spent and where you spent it. This is critical information when building your personal income statement. If all your transactions are on a credit card, then at year end, you can download your transactions and easily create your personal income statement. However, a debit card will also allow you to do this. So again, if the reason you are using a credit card is for record keeping—Stop! You will get all the benefits you are looking for without any of the drawbacks associated with ugly debt.

Rewards

Rewards are one reason I can think of to use a credit card. Many credit card companies offer rewards of some kind for using their card, with the most popular rewards being in the form of cash back or travel benefits. This is a permissible use for using a credit card. However, there are three caveats.

First, you need to do a cost-benefit analysis. If you are using a credit card that has a $120 annual fee, but you're only getting $50 worth of benefits in cash back or travel benefits, you are making a mistake. Do not do this. Always compare the cost of the card to the value you are receiving. If the cost exceeds the benefit, do not get the credit card.

Second, you must be disciplined enough to pay off your credit card on time every month. Never carry a balance. If you carry a balance, you have turned your credit card into ugly debt, and ugly debt is never a good thing. Some people live a month ahead of themselves. They incur credit card debt today, without the cash to pay it off, knowing that next month they will get paid and have the funds to pay off the credit card. This is extremely dangerous. If you do not have the cash in your account to pay off the amount charged, you should not be using a credit card. Planning to use your income earned tomorrow to pay off a credit card charge of today is simply borrowing from the future. This will never turn out well.

Third, even if you pay off your credit card each month, you must ask yourself, Do I spend more than I otherwise would because of the credit card? This is a hidden cost of credit cards that almost everyone ignores. If your credit card tempts you to spend more, you must factor that additional spending into your cost-benefit analysis.

Online Purchases
Online purchases are another area where it makes sense to use a credit card.

First, you cannot even make an online purchase without providing either a credit card or a debit card.

Second, if for any reason you have problems with your purchase, the credit card company will sometimes step in and refund your purchase and charge it back to the vendor. Thus, using a credit card can add a level of online security. However, the same caveat for rewards applies here. You must be disciplined enough to pay off your credit card on time every month. Never carry a balance. If you carry a balance, you have turned a credit card into ugly debt, and ugly debt is never a good thing.

One final word about credit cards: If you have not learned to manage your debt, never use a credit card. Never.

Cost of Credit Cards
To help you understand the cost of a credit card and why you must never carry a balance, I have done some simple math for you. According to the Experian 2020 Consumer Credit Review, the average credit card balance as of December 31, 2020 is approximately $5,313. Further, according to creditcards.com, as of July 2021, the lowest credit card interest rate is 12.96%, the average interest rate is 16.16%, and the highest interest rate is 25.05%. These rates will regularly fluctuate, and every card will be different, but I will use these numbers for an illustrative example.

The following table summarizes how long it will take to pay off $5,313 worth of charges to your credit card, provided you regularly make the minimum monthly payment.

Interest Rate	Time to Pay Off	Total Payments($)	Total Interest($)
12.96%	18 years, 1 month	10,255	4.942
16.16%	18 years, 8 months	11,562	6,249
25.05%	20 years, 2 months	15,268	9,955

These numbers tell the whole story. Using the average outstanding balance and the average credit card interest rate, if all you do is make the minimum monthly payment, it will take almost 19 years to pay off the credit card. The interest charges actually exceed the outstanding amount. This means everything you bought and charged to your credit card is literally costing you more than two times what you paid for it.

Think about that the next time you want to purchase something using your credit card. Can you really afford to pay two times the asking price? This is why debt, and in particular credit card debt, is to be avoided. It is an absolute slayer of wealth and the mother of untold tears, grief, pain, and stress. Need I say more?

Key Takeaways:
 1. **Debt is a horrible master.**
 2. **Get out of debt as soon as you can.**
 3. **Avoid ugly debt at all costs.**
 4. **Bad and ugly debts are the slayers of wealth and the mother of tears.**

15

HELP! I AM ALREADY IN DEBT

If you are like most people, there are two true statements about your life:

1. You are already in debt.
2. You wish you were not in debt.

If those statements ring true, then this chapter is for you. There is an adage that I learned long ago: "If you find yourself in a hole, stop digging." Nothing could be truer in managing our finances.

If you find yourself in a financial hole, the first thing you need to do is stop digging. In other words, if you find yourself in debt, the first thing you need to do is to stop incurring more debt. You need to stop digging. That is why the first few chapters of this book discussed exactly that—how to stop digging. You stop digging by building a budget and getting your finances back under your control. You start to live by the Rule of Financial Happiness by making sure your cash inflows exceed your cash outflows.

However, once you have stopped digging, you still have a hole you need to fill. For some people, it appears to be a formidable task. A gigantic hole the size of the Grand Canyon. How do you fill such a hole? First, let me assure you, it is possible. It has been done countless times by countless others, but it does take a plan, and it does take discipline and patience. Let me share with you a few thoughts on how to fill the hole. I would suggest taking the following steps:

1. Calculate Your "Real Debt"
2. Create a Debt Calendar
3. Attack the Debt

Calculate Your Real Debt

The first thing I would do is calculate my real debt. What do I mean by real debt? Well, there is a difference between the *principal* and the total amount owed. The *principal* is the amount borrowed. When people think of their debt, they usually think of the amount borrowed, but that is not the real debt. The real debt is the sum of payments you must make to pay off the debt. That is, the real debt is the total of all the principal payments, plus the interest payments.

In the last chapter, I discussed credit card debt and how long it would take to pay that off. In the example I provided, the amount borrowed was $5,313, but if you only make the minimum payment, using the average interest rate of 16.16%, the real debt is $11,562. That is because even though someone only "borrowed" $5,313, by incurring those charges on their credit card, and only making the minimum payments, they will have to pay $11,562 to pay the debt off. Thus, the real debt is $11,562, not $5,313. Credit card companies do not want you to understand this because this is what generates profits for them. Though, unfortunately, their profit is your misery. Thus, the first step is to understand your real debt. Figure out what your monthly payment is and for how many months you must make that payment. Multiply the monthly payment by the number of months outstanding, and you will have your real debt. Do that calculation for each of your debts.

Create a Debt Calendar

Once you have calculated your real debt, create a debt calendar. You can do this by creating a spreadsheet (or taking a piece of paper), and across the top, write down each of your creditors, the monthly payment, and the interest rate you are being charged. Along the side, write down the number of months. Then for each month, under each creditor, write in the monthly payment. Your schedule should look something like this. (Note: If you are only making the minimum payment on your credit cards, the actual number of months and the actual real debt will be substantially higher. For simplicity, I have chosen to show the credit card debt being paid off over three years and two years respectively).

Buy the Milk First

Table 1: Sample Debt Calendar

Month	Credit Card 1 3,458 18%	Credit Card 2 5,674 24%	Car Loan 6,764 8%	Furniture 2,844 10%	Medical 711 6%	Total 19,451
1	125	300	400	250	180	1,255
2	125	300	400	250	180	1,255
3	125	300	400	250	180	1,255
4	125	300	400	250	180	1,255
5	125	300	400	250		1,075
6	125	300	400	250		1,075
7	125	300	400	250		1,075
8	125	300	400	250		1,075
9	125	300	400	250		1,075
10	125	300	400	250		1,075
11	125	300	400	250		1,075
12	125	300	400	250		1,075
13	125	300	400			825
14	125	300	400			825
15	125	300	400			825
16	125	300	400			825
17	125	300	400			825
18	125	300	400			825
19	125	300				425
20	125	300				425
21	125	300				425
22	125	300				425
23	125	300				425
24	125	300				425
25	125					125
26	125					125
27	125					125
28	125					125
29	125					125
30	125					125
31	125					125
32	125					125
33	125					125
34	125					125
35	125					125
36	125					125
Total Real Debt	4,500	7,200	7,200	3,000	720	22,620

The advantage of the calendar is that it allows you to not only visually see exactly what your payments are, but you can also see the light at the end of the tunnel. You can easily see in this calendar that after four months, there is a little bit of light once the medical bill is paid off. Then there is additional light after 12 months when the furniture loan is paid off. This should start to give you hope and help you realize that you can pull this off. Now comes the fun part where you can supercharge your debt paydown. You do that by attacking the debt.

Attack the Debt

A passive response to debt would be living with the debt paydown calendar you created. Based on this calendar, that means you are debt-free in 36 months. However, you can do better. Much better. The trick, once you have stopped digging a hole, is to be disciplined and focused. You want to get rid of the evil taskmaster of debt and take control back. This is how you do it.

First, notice that the medical debt was paid off after four months. This frees up an additional $180/month in our budget. We can choose to allocate this money elsewhere in our budget, such as for more entertainment, or we can choose to supercharge our debt paydown. I strongly encourage you to supercharge. That means you take the $180 and instead of using it to increase your discretionary spending, you apply it to other debt payments and pay them off faster.

The order in which you complete the supercharge is not as important as the concept of the supercharge. Some people like the idea of applying the additional $180 to the debt with the shortest life. The advantage to this system is it builds psychological positivity. It is a great feeling when a debt is finally paid off, and it creates motivation to continue with the plan and attack the other debts. If you think you could use some motivation to keep you going, this is a great system. Others like to attack the debt with the highest interest rate first. The advantage of this system is it reduces the total amount of real debt, as the total interest paid is diminished. If you do not need the psychological reinforcement of eliminating debt payments and just want to reduce the total interest costs, then this may be the preferred option.

The key is to supercharge the debt paydown by taking the extra funds created by paying off one debt and applying those funds to accelerate the payoff of another debt. Do not, I repeat, do not take those funds and add them to discretionary spending. We need to slay the monster called debt and reclaim our freedom as fast as we can. That means we need to supercharge our debt payments.

There is also a third and enormously powerful way to supercharge the debt payments. As you live within your budget and get more disciplined, you may find that there are other expenses you can cut out. You may have budgeted for having a coffee every day at Starbucks. However, you now have realized you do not need to go to Starbucks every day. In this situation, you have freed up a few more funds. If that happens, do not spend the money elsewhere—instead, supercharge your debt paydown and use that money to pay off your debt. You will be surprised by how fast it adds up. Finally, as time goes by, you may find yourself with more income. Perhaps you got a raise. If so, do not spend the extra money. Supercharge your debt paydown. The faster you slay the debt monster, the sooner you regain control of your life.

Finally, there is one more way to attack the debt: lowering your interest rate. If you can lower your interest rate, you will have automatically reduced the amount of real debt. The reduced interest will free up more funds to attack the debt even faster. There are a few ways you can reduce your interest rate.

The first is rather obvious. Some of your existing creditors, such as banks, may be willing to reduce the interest rate simply by you asking. Alternatively, a new lender may be willing to offer a lower interest rate. If you have credit card debt, you can transfer your debt to a different credit card with a lower interest rate. If you own your home and have a mortgage, have mortgage rates dropped such that you can refinance your home and get a lower interest rate? With a little creative thinking, and little bit of leg work, you will be surprised at how you can lower your real debt.

I have created two more tables to help you visualise the power of supercharging your debt paydown.

Table 2: Attack First the Debt with the Shortest Maturity

Principal Month	Credit Card 1 3,458 18%	Credit Card 2 5,674 24%	Car Loan 6,764 8%	Furniture 2,844 10%	Medical 711 6%	Total 19,451
1	125	300	400	250	180	1,255
2	125	300	400	250	180	1,255
3	125	300	400	250	180	1,255
4	125	300	400	250	180	1,255
5	125	300	400	430		1,255
6	125	300	400	430		1,255
7	125	300	400	430		1,255
8	125	300	400	430		1,255
9	125	300	578	252		1,255
10	125	300	830			1,255
11	125	300	830			1,255
12	125	300	830			1,255
13	125	300	830			1,255
14	125	1089	41			1,255
15	125	1130				1,255
16	425	830				1,255
17	1255					1,255
18	628					628
19						-
20						-
21						-
22						-
23						-
24						-
25						-
26						-
27						-
28						-
29						-
30						-
31						-
32						-
33						-
34						-
35						-
36						-
Total Real Debt	4,183	6,949	7,139	2,972	720	21,963

Table 2 shows what happens if you supercharge your debt payments by applying the funds created from one debt payoff to the next shortest debt payoff. You can see that supercharging your debt moves you from being debt-free in 36 months to being debt-free in 18 months. You have cut the amount of time in half. Further, you have reduced your real debt from $22,620 to $21,963. A saving of $657! That is money straight from your creditor's pocket into your own pocket for doing nothing more than staying disciplined and supercharging your debt.

Table 3: Attack First the Debt with the Highest Interest Rate

Principal Month	Credit Card 1 3,458 18%	Credit Card 2 5,674 24%	Car Loan 6,764 8%	Furniture 2,844 10%	Medical 711 6%	Total 19,451
1	125	300	400	250	180	1,255
2	125	300	400	250	180	1,255
3	125	300	400	250	180	1,255
4	125	300	400	250	180	1,255
5	125	480	400	250		1,255
6	125	480	400	250		1,255
7	125	480	400	250		1,255
8	125	480	400	250		1,255
9	125	480	400	250		1,255
10	125	480	400	250		1,255
11	125	480	400	250		1,255
12	125	480	400	250		1,255
13	125	730	400			1,255
14	125	730	400			1,255
15	632	223	400			1,255
16	855		400			1,255
17	855		400			1,255
18	61		400			461
19						-
20						-
21						-
22						-
23						-
24						-
25						-
26						-
27						-
28						-
29						-
30						-
31						-
32						-
33						-
34						-
35						-
36						-
Total Real Debt	4,153	6,723	7,200	3,000	720	21,796

Table 3 shows what happens if you take the funds created from one debt payoff and apply it to the debt with the highest interest rate. You can see in this table that you are still debt-free in 18 months, and you have reduced your real debt to $21,796. A saving of $824 or by an additional $167 versus applying the payments to shortest debt payoff. The additional $167 is the interest savings you created by applying the extra funds to the debt with the highest interest rate.

Note that in both scenarios you can cut your countdown to freedom by half. Thus, choose whichever attack method you want, and that will keep you motivated. Both methods work fine but do make sure you supercharge your debt. Supercharging your debt is like bringing a gun to a knife fight. It is the fastest way to slay the monster and regain control of your life.

Key Takeaways:
    1. Calculate Your "Real Debt."
    2. Create a Debt Calendar.
    3. Attack the Debt.

PART IV

PERFORMING THE PLAN

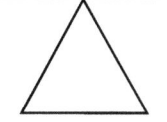

16

THE DYNAMIC DUO—THE SECRETS TO WEALTH CREATION

Congratulations! You have now taken control of your financial life. You are now in control, as opposed to being controlled. You have applied the principles in this book; you are living within your means. Your cash inflows exceed your cash outflows, and your debt is totally under control. With that as a foundation, you are now ready to start building your wealth. Wealth building is not as difficult or as scary as many people think. It simply requires the knowledge and application of two simple principles. Individually, each principle is simple yet powerful, but when combined they become life-changing. They are like putting jet packs on your financial shoulders—that is why I call them the Dynamic Duo.

I would venture that most people believe that to create wealth you either need to be an entrepreneur who starts up a successful company or be someone with a large income. Fortunately, neither is true.

We are all familiar with the story of some Internet entrepreneur who invested everything they had into an original business concept and then became a billionaire. This story is great, and good for them! I have never begrudged one nickel of any entrepreneur who starts up a business and becomes extremely successful. They only get there by making life better for countless others, so we should all be grateful to them. However, those wealth stories are rare. To use that as our pattern for creating wealth would just be foolish. It would be like expecting every child who ever picked up a basketball to grow up and be the next Michael Jordon or LeBron James. It is just not going to happen. This is not something we can all do to create wealth.

The other way people think that wealth is created is through a large income. The theory is that the larger the income, the greater the wealth creation. However, this theory is also false. There are many people who have large incomes but have never created wealth.

In the Preface I mentioned the conversation I had with the wife of a successful dentist. Despite having a large income, they had still had financial problems and had to hire an accounting firm to help manage their personal finances. I also had another client that I knew quite well. I was helping this client to sell their business and move to another country. This client had all the appearances of wealth. A successful business, a nice home, a nice car, even a vacation property on a lake. However, as I got into the details of the personal financial situation, I was surprised to learn that this client had no wealth. After selling all the assets, the client barely had enough for a modest down payment on a home. Again, even though the client generated excellent income, the client did not create wealth. Sadly, there are many examples like this one. Having a large income does not guarantee the creation of wealth. While a large income is certainly helpful, it is not necessary, and it is absolutely not the single most important factor in creating wealth.

Net Investible Income

The single most important factor in creating wealth—and the first of our Dynamic Duo principles—is *net investible income*. Net investible income is not your gross income. Net investible income is the amount of money you have left after subtracting your expenses from your income. It is a subtle yet significant difference. The amount of money you can put into your savings and investment accounts while still running a surplus in your budget is what matters. In other words, it is not your gross income that matters; it is your net income that matters. If you are making one million dollars a year, but you are spending one million and one dollars a year, you will never create wealth. You might have the appearance of wealth, but you, in fact, will have no wealth.

A 2009 *Sports Illustrated* article stated that 78% of former NFL players have gone bankrupt or are under financial stress and that an estimated 60%

of former NBA players are broke within 5 years of retirement. Clearly, a large income is not the key to creating wealth. I am sure there are several reasons why all those professional athletes ran into money problems, but one thing is quite clear. Their cash outflows (expenses) exceeded their cash inflows (income). They had no investible income. Investible income is the key. It is the single most important factor in creating wealth. The higher the investible income, the quicker wealth can be created.

Creating investible income is simply getting back to the basics. Establish a budget, live within your means, increase income, and decrease expenses. It is not rocket science. It is about knowing and applying the most basic financial laws to your life. Nonetheless, even though net investible income is the single most important factor in creating wealth, it needs the right partner to truly become life changing.

Compounding

The second principle of the Dynamic Duo—and the catalyst for making net investible income life-changing—is the law of *compounding*. Compounding is when you are earning income in the current year on top of the income you earned in prior years. For example, let's say you invest $1,000 and earn 10% a year. At the end of the first year, you would have $1,100. The $1,000 you invested, plus $100 of income ($100 being 10% of the $1,000). However, at the end of the second year, you would have $1,210. The $1,100 from the end of year one, plus $100 of income on the original $1,000 you invested, plus $10 of income from the $100 you earned in year one. The additional $10 of income is the compounded income for one year, and each year that number gets bigger and bigger.

As you start earning income on top of your income, the results can be staggering. In fact, Albert Einstein has been credited with saying, "Compound interest is the most powerful force in the universe." He is also credited with saying, "Compound interest is the 8th wonder of the world. He who understands it, earns it. He who doesn't, pays it." I am not sure if Einstein said those words, but he could have. They are based on brilliant and true mathematical and financial laws.

Let's see what happens when you apply the principle of compounding with time, assuming you invest $1,000 and earn 10% per year on that $1,000.

(The 10% is the stock market average return for 30 years ending December 31, 2019.) After just over 7 years, that initial $1,000 will have earned you an additional $1,000. How much would the $1,000 have earned you after 70 years (which is 10 times 7 years)? Would the amount earned also be 10 times more or $10,000? Well, through the magical power of compounding, you would have earned just under $790,000. In the first year, you would earn $100, but in the 70th year, when you earn income on prior years' income, you would then earn $72,000. That is the power of compounding!

I was first introduced to the power of compounding when, as a young child, I was asked whether I would rather have a million dollars or a penny that doubled every day for 30 days. If you do not stop to think, many people will say a million dollars. They would be so wrong. A single penny that doubles every day for 30 days would be worth close to 11 million dollars. That is compounding. However, both these examples are a little extreme. No one invests $1,000 today and then waits 70 years. And no one doubles their money every day.

Let's use an example that is much more realistic. Let's compare two sisters: Wise Wendy and Silly Sally.

Wise Wendy is very disciplined in her early years. Starting with when she turns 20, Wise Wendy creates her budget and comes up with $2,000 a year of net investible income. She invests $2,000 on her birthday every year for 10 years and then never invests again. Her sister, Silly Sally, invests the same amount starting when she turns 30, but she keeps investing for 35 years. Both sisters earn a market average return of 10% per year. (The 10% rate is based on the S&P 500 average return for the 30-year period ending December 31, 2019. The S&P 500 is an index of the 500 largest U.S. publicly traded companies. Thus, the 10% rate of return is based on the 30-year average rate of return of the 500 largest U.S. publicly traded companies.) What does each sister's account look like when they turn 65?

Table 4: Wise Wendy vs. Silly Sally

Wise Wendy

Age	Beginning Account Value	Amount Invested	Average Rate of Return	Income	Ending Account Value
20	0	2,000	10%	200	2,200
21	2,200	2,000	10%	420	4,620
22	4,620	2,000	10%	662	7,282
23	7,282	2,000	10%	928	10,210
24	10,210	2,000	10%	1,221	13,431
25	13,431	2,000	10%	1,543	16,974
26	16,974	2,000	10%	1,897	20,872
27	20,872	2,000	10%	2,287	25,159
28	25,159	2,000	10%	2,716	29,875
29	29,875	2,000	10%	3,187	35,062
30	35,062	0	10%	3,506	38,569
31	38,569	0	10%	3,857	42,425
32	42,425	0	10%	4,243	46,668
33	46,668	0	10%	4,667	51,335
34	51,335	0	10%	5,133	56,468
35	56,468	0	10%	5,647	62,115
36	62,115	0	10%	6,212	68,327
37	68,327	0	10%	6,833	75,159
38	75,159	0	10%	7,516	82,675
39	82,675	0	10%	8,268	90,943
40	90,943	0	10%	9,094	100,037
41	100,037	0	10%	10,004	110,041
42	110,041	0	10%	11,004	121,045

Wise Wendy

Age	Beginning Account Value	Amount Invested	Average Rate of Return	Income	Ending Account Value
43	121,045	0	10%	12,104	133,149
44	133,149	0	10%	13,315	146,464
45	146,464	0	10%	14,646	161,110
46	161,110	0	10%	16,111	177,222
47	177,222	0	10%	17,722	194,944
48	194,944	0	10%	19,494	214,438
49	214,438	0	10%	21,444	235,882
50	235,882	0	10%	23,588	259,470
51	259,470	0	10%	25,947	285,417
52	285,417	0	10%	28,542	313,959
53	313,959	0	10%	31,396	345,355
54	345,355	0	10%	34,535	379,890
55	379,890	0	10%	37,989	417,879
56	417,879	0	10%	41,788	459,667
57	459,667	0	10%	45,967	505,634
58	505,634	0	10%	50,563	556,197
59	556,197	0	10%	55,620	611,817
60	611,817	0	10%	61,182	672,998
61	672,998	0	10%	67,300	740,298
62	740,298	0	10%	74,030	814,328
63	814,328	0	10%	81,433	895,761
64	895,761	0	10%	89,576	985,337
65	**985,337**				

Buy the Milk First

Silly Sally

Age	Beginning Account Value	Amount Invested	Average Rate of Return	Income	Ending Account Value
20	0	0	10%	0	0
21	0	0	10%	0	0
22	0	0	10%	0	0
23	0	0	10%	0	0
24	0	0	10%	0	0
25	0	0	10%	0	0
26	0	0	10%	0	0
27	0	0	10%	0	0
28	0	0	10%	0	0
29	0	0	10%	0	0
30	0	2,000	10%	200	2,200
31	2,200	2,000	10%	420	4,620
32	4,620	2,000	10%	662	7,282
33	7,282	2,000	10%	928	10,210
34	10,210	2,000	10%	1,221	13,431
35	13,431	2,000	10%	1,543	16,974
36	16,974	2,000	10%	1,897	20,872
37	20,872	2,000	10%	2,287	25,159
38	25,159	2,000	10%	2,716	29,875
39	29,875	2,000	10%	3,187	35,062
40	35,062	2,000	10%	3,706	40,769
41	40,769	2,000	10%	4,277	47,045
42	47,045	2,000	10%	4,905	53,950
43	53,950	2,000	10%	5,595	61,545

Murray J Lee

Silly Sally

Age	Beginning Account Value	Amount Invested	Average Rate of Return	Income	Ending Account Value
44	61,545	2,000	10%	6,354	69,899
45	69,899	2,000	10%	7,190	79,089
46	79,089	2,000	10%	8,109	89,198
47	89,198	2,000	10%	9,120	100,318
48	100,318	2,000	10%	10,232	112,550
49	112,550	2,000	10%	11,455	126,005
50	126,005	2,000	10%	12,800	140,805
51	140,805	2,000	10%	14,281	157,086
52	157,086	2,000	10%	15,909	174,995
53	174,995	2,000	10%	17,699	194,694
54	194,694	2,000	10%	19,669	216,364
55	216,364	2,000	10%	21,836	240,200
56	240,200	2,000	10%	24,220	266,420
57	266,420	2,000	10%	26,842	295,262
58	295,262	2,000	10%	29,726	326,988
59	326,988	2,000	10%	32,899	361,887
60	361,887	2,000	10%	36,389	400,276
61	400,276	2,000	10%	40,228	442,503
62	442,503	2,000	10%	44,450	488,953
63	488,953	2,000	10%	49,095	540,049
64	540,049	2,000	10%	54,205	596,254
65	**596,254**				

Buy the Milk First

Wise Wendy has contributed $20,000 into her account—$2,000 per year for 10 years, and then never again. Silly Sally, on the other hand, waited until she was a bit more established. She waited 10 extra years to start, but then she has faithfully contributed $2,000 a year for 35 years. A total $70,000 investment (or $50,000) more than her sister, Wise Wendy. Yet, at age 65, Silly Sally still has less in her retirement account than Wise Wendy. Wise Wendy will have around $985,000 while Silly Sally will have around $596,000. Silly Sally has earned just over $7.5 for every dollar invested. This is not bad, but Wise Wendy, who started sooner—despite quitting investing and letting the power of compounding continue its work—earned just over $48 for every dollar invested. Over six times more than Silly Sally. This is the power of compounding.

However, there is one more factor at play here. Patience. Think of compounding as a snowball rolling down the hill. The further it gets down the hill, the faster the snowball grows. It is the same with compounding. The more time we allow compounding to work, the more effective and powerful it becomes. Each year it becomes exponentially more powerful than the prior year. In the case of Wise Wendy, almost 62% of her entire $965,000 profit came in the last 10 years. In the case of Silly Sally, just over 68% of her entire $526,000 profit came in the last 10 years. Thus, while compounding is an extremely powerful force, it gains its power through the momentum of time. The more time you allow the power of compounding to work, the more powerful it becomes.

You now understand both principles of the Dynamic Duo. The principle of net investible income and the principle of compounding. Now imagine putting those two forces together and the life-changing impact it can have. Now you're putting on the jet packs!

Let's go back to Wise Wendy's income, and let's say that for the first 10 years she was able to scrimp and save and find another $2,000 a year of net investible income. She invested $4,000 a year for 10 years instead of $2,000 a year for 10 years (or an additional $20,000 in total). At age 65, she would be sitting on an additional $985,000 or close to two million dollars in total. This would be life-changing, and it's all because she applied both principles together.

Net investible income is critical to wealth creation, but the financial law of compounding is the game-changing multiplier. These two forces, working together, are truly a Dynamic Duo. The lesson here is simple. To create wealth, you need to maximize your net investible income as early as you can and then be patient and let the power of compounding work for you. You will be amazed at what this can do for you.

Key Takeaways:
1. **Net investible income is the single most important factor in wealth creation.**
2. **Compounding is an incredibly powerful force that acts as a multiplier to net investible income.**
3. **Net investible income, combined with compounding, forms an unbeatable and life-changing Dynamic Duo.**
4. **The sooner you create net investible income, the more powerful is the multiplying force of compounding.**

17

YOUR FINANCIAL PERSONAL FLOTATION DEVICE

As you contemplate your investment decisions, it's important to remember a few more key principles. In this chapter, I want to talk about the *3 Be's* of investing. Every great investor has applied the *3 Be* principles. It would be wise for you to apply them as well. They are:

1. Be **P**atient
2. Be **F**ocused
3. Be **D**iligent

Think of these *3 Be's* as your investing PFD or "Personal Flotation Device." Applying these principles will help you stay afloat in a sea of financial storms.

Be Patient
When I say be patient, I mean that in two vastly different ways. The first is with respect to time. Every great investor understands the multiplier effect of compounding. They are not looking for a get-rich-quick scheme. They understand that compounding takes time, and the more time they give it, the exponentially more powerful the principle of compounding becomes. You do not have to hit a home run on every investment. You can be a champion investor just by hitting singles and doubles.

In 2003, Michael Lewis wrote a book called, *Moneyball: The Art of Winning an Unfair Game*. A film adaptation of the book, also titled *Moneyball*, was released in 2011. The movie and the book were about the Oakland Athletics baseball team and their 2002 season. That year, the Oakland Athletics won their division but perhaps more famously had a record-setting 20-game winning streak. However, the real story is how they did it. They had a total player salary of close to one-third of the major markets, yet they still managed to win their division. One of the great keys to their success, which has now been duplicated by other professional sport teams, is they looked for the undervalued players. They did not look for the players with the big home run records or players who stole a lot of bases; they looked for the players who simply got on base. Whether it was a walk or a single hit, it did not matter. Just get on base.

The Oakland Athletics' theory was that the market overvalued (i.e., overpaid) players who were the big home run hitters or base stealers and undervalued (i.e., discounted) players who quietly got the job done by simply getting on base. They analyzed the data and figured that the guy who stole a lot of bases, and added extra runs because of it, also lost a lot of runs because he was sometimes thrown out trying to steal a base. Same with the home run hitters—even though they got a lot of home runs, they also struck out a lot because they were searching for the home run pitch. The Oakland Athletics determined that they would win more games if they gave up the big winning plays of home runs and stolen bases in exchange for giving up the losing plays of being thrown out stealing a base or striking out at the plate. They further realized that the players who quietly got it done were undervalued.

Putting those two tidbits of information together, they theorized that they could sign the undervalued players, keep their payroll costs down, and still produce a winning team. Their theory worked. They were in the bottom two of payrolls that year and yet had one of the highest winning percentages—ultimately winning their division. This is the kind of stuff they make movies about!

You can apply the same principle in your investing. When you first start investing, do not look for the home runs. Be patient, be happy, and look for the singles. Several singles are better than a home run, especially when you realize you have the power of compounding. Small singles, combined with compounding, will still be life changing. Be patient. Let compounding do the work.

Buy the Milk First

That brings us to the second meaning behind being patient: the "Bus Principle." The Bus Principle simply means that there is always another bus coming. Do not rush to make an investment. Be patient. To continue with our baseball analogy, you do not have to swing at every pitch. Wait for the fat pitch; wait for the opportunity that makes sense and that you are comfortable with. Do not let a smooth-talking salesperson convince you to invest. Some of your best investments will be the ones you do not even make. Remember, investments are like buses—there is always another one coming. Be patient.

Be Focused
Part of being a good investor is being focused. As you are trying to create wealth, you will be tempted to loosen the purse strings and splurge a little. This is where you need to be focused. Remember that one of the 3 Ps is prioritize and ask yourself, Is this expenditure consistent with the priorities I have set for myself? If not, then stay focused and pass on the expense. This is particularly important to remember as your income increases. Too many people increase their income and then immediately increase their expenses. It is extremely difficult to create wealth if your spending increases every time your income increases.

Remember the cardinal rule of priorities: Never let a lower priority take precedence over a higher priority. Never. An increase in income does not equate to a change in priorities. If your priorities have not changed, then your spending should not change. An increase in income should be applied towards an increase in your savings account or an increase in your investment account. This is the best way to create wealth. This principle is easy in concept but difficult in practice. This is where self-discipline is important.

I have a friend who decided early in his career that investing in condominiums would be his path to becoming a multi-millionaire and independently wealthy. Every time he looked at a particularly large expenditure, like buying a car, he would ask himself, Would I rather make this big purchase or buy a condominium? He always chose to buy a condominium and indeed became a multi-millionaire because of it. In fact, it has now been several years since he achieved that status, and to this day, I do not believe he has ever bought a new car. He knows how he got there, and he does not see any reason to change. Stay focused on your goals. Once you finally achieve them, you will be glad you did.

Another way to be focused is finding a system that works for you. My friend chose real estate, as it was an industry that he was comfortable with and that worked for him. That was his system, but it is not the only system. I know a venture capitalist who would raise money from investors and then invest that money, on their behalf, in various private companies, which were later sold or went public. He learned to analyze companies in detail, spot opportunities or companies that were undervalued, and then invest. He has long since retired from the venture capital business, but he now applies those same skills in his own time, as he looks in the public market for publicly traded companies that are undervalued and invests. He generates capital gains through his investing and then sells his investments at a profit to support himself. It is within his comfort zone, and it works for him.

Personally, I do not look primarily for capital gains. I look for stable dividend paying companies with a history of consistently paying dividends to their shareholders. I like the idea of getting a regular dividend because if I were to die tomorrow, I would leave my family with an income stream from which they can live off. Looking for solid dividend-paying companies has worked for me.

I have another friend who owns a successful private company. Every time he looks at an investment, whether it be in rental real estate, the stock market, or elsewhere, he says to himself, Why would I do this? Can I get a better return on my investment by investing in this or by investing in and growing my own company instead? He usually invests in his own company.

No one system is necessarily better or worse than another. All are successful, all have achieved their priorities, and all are different. My friend who invests in real estate would be uncomfortable investing in the public markets, and he probably would not be as successful. One reason they are all successful is they all know what they do know and what they do not know. And they stick to what they do know. They stay disciplined and do not stray. The point is, do not try to become an expert in everything, and do not invest in what you do not know. There are many correct paths, but you need to choose your path. You cannot be all things to all people. Stay focused.

Be Diligent

The last *Be* of investing is to be diligent. Do your homework. It is surprising to me how often people will spend hours and hours of research when considering buying a new car, but they will make an investment without doing any research or, worse, based on a rumour or a "tip" from a friend. This is a recipe for disaster. When you are making an investment, you are taking your hard-earned dollars and asking them to now go to work for you. In effect, you have converted each dollar into a little employee. Each dollar now works for you, and you need to protect those little employees and make sure that each one is both safe and productive. The best way to ensure this happens is to do your homework. Ask questions. Make sure you understand the risks and the benefits. Is this an area in which you are knowledgeable? Is the management hard-working, experienced, and reputable? Do you understand your alternatives? Is there a better place to invest? Ask lots of questions to make sure you are both knowledgeable and comfortable. If you cannot get there, then pass.

Remember the "Bus Principle." There will always be another opportunity. If you do not have the time to do your due diligence, then pass on the opportunity. You are much better off to not make an investment than to make an investment in which you have not done your due diligence. Failure to make an investment now means you still have a chance to make an investment later. Making an investment without proper diligence usually means you lose your investment. Be wise in your investing. Do your due diligence. As I said before, sometimes the best investments are the investments that were never made. If you are not comfortable, do not invest.

Key Takeaways:
The *3 Be*'s of Investing:
1. **Be Patient—remember the "Bus Principle."**
2. **Be Focused.**
3. **Be Diligent.**

18

THE FOUR "DO" LAWS OF INVESTING

There are four "Do" laws of investing that every successful investor strives for. They are:

1. Do Get a Little Richer Every Day.
2. Do Invest in Yourself through Education.
3. Do Build Your Balance Sheet.
4. Do Manage Risk.

If you want to create wealth, you will need to learn to do each of the above four items. While there are many other options that you can pursue, these four are the building blocks that you need to start with.

Do Get a Little Richer Every Day
You need to set a goal for yourself that each day you will get a little richer. If you make this commitment to yourself, it will change the way you think, the way you act, and the way you feel. Adopting this simple goal, and combining it with the superpower of compounding, can be life-changing. Let's say you decide to get richer each day by at least $10. Each day you take $10 and transfer it to your investment account. If you earn a compounded rate of return of 5% and start doing this at the age of 25, by the time you are 65 you will have just over $466,000! If you invest at 10%, you would have just under two million dollars! At $15 a day, with a 10% compounded return,

you will have over 2.9 million dollars. These are staggering and life-changing numbers, and it all starts with a simple goal to get a little richer every day.

If you adopt this plan, a few other advantages will occur. You will feel less stressed about the future. You will know you have a very workable plan in place that will allow you to not only retire, but to retire in comfort. You will think more about taking on unnecessary risk and thus, you will become much better at managing risk. You will start to get excited about what you are building, and you will suddenly find it easier to transfer a little more to your investment account each day. You will think different, you will act different, and you will feel different. Set the goal. Get a little richer each day. You will be amazed by the results.

Do Invest in Yourself through Education

If you think education is expensive, try ignorance. One of, if not *the* best investment you can make, is to invest in yourself. Investing in yourself can result in huge returns.

Think of a lawyer, an accountant, or a physician. All these people made investments in themselves when they were younger that allowed them to earn much more income later. The same is true for the trades. Plumbers and electricians have made investments in themselves, and because of those investments, they are able to earn substantially more income than they otherwise would.

Formal education is not the only form of investing in yourself. Read books, attend seminars, and subscribe to newsletters. All of these are various forms of keeping yourself educated. A couple of years after graduating university, I enrolled in a real estate course offered at the local junior college. The course was offered over a few weekends. In the course, I learned some basic real estate law, such as the laws that governed the paying of commission to real estate agents. I also learned that, in the state in which I resided, attorneys automatically qualified as real estate agents and could receive a commission on the sale of a home. That one single piece of information was worth more than the cost of the course.

As a recently graduated university student, I did not have the cash needed for a down payment on a house. I thought buying a house would have to wait. However, with that one piece of information from the course, I realized

I could walk into a model home and list my attorney friend as my real estate agent. That entitled my friend to receive the commission on the sale of the house, which he had agreed to give back to me. Suddenly, with the money I had, plus the realtor's commission on the purchase of my house, I had the required down payment, and I bought my first home. All because I invested in my own education. As a side note, I mentioned this little trick to three of my friends who all used the same tactic to purchase their first homes as well.

As the years have gone by, and my investment account has increased, I started buying stocks in the stock market. To educate myself, I began subscribing to various investment newsletters. Newsletters that are subscription-based, not commission-based. As I read these newsletters, I became a better investor. While in terms of actual dollars the newsletters could be considered expensive, they have paid me back the cost multiple times by making me a better investor and providing me with ideas that I would not have discovered on my own. Ignorance is much more expensive than education. Invest in your education.

Do Build Your Balance Sheet
Every accountant knows that a set of financial statements includes different types of statements. Of the different types of statements, many people focus exclusively on the income statement, which we covered in Chapter 11. The income statement shows your revenue and expenses over a period of time (for one year or for one month). Many investors think this is the only statement that matters. They could not be more wrong.

And in the area of personal finance, most people do not even write up a personal income statement. For those who do write a personal income statement, they believe that's the only statement needed, but an income statement is only one part of the financial statement package. Another part is the balance sheet.

Understanding your balance sheet is critical. If you ignore the balance sheet, you do so at your peril. Sophisticated investors spend a lot of time on the balance sheet. This should be no different when it comes to our personal finances.

While an income statement highlights your revenue and expenses over a period of time, a balance sheet provides you with a snapshot, at a specific point in time, of your assets, your liabilities (debt), and your equity (net worth). It is the scorecard that lets you know if your plan is working or needs adjusting. It is through your balance sheet that you will know if you are ready to weather a financial storm. It is like a lighthouse warning ships of impending danger.

Every year, thousands and thousands of individuals and businesses file for bankruptcy. I suspect not one of those bankrupt individuals or businesses had a strong balance sheet. Every one of them could have been like a ship, adjusting course due to the warning lights of the lighthouse. They just had to look. Had they looked, they could have seen the bankruptcy ahead and adjusted course. Many of them could have avoided the bankruptcy if they had paid attention to their balance sheet.

You must constantly look at your balance sheet and ask yourself, Are my assets growing faster than my liabilities (debts)? By assets, I do not mean toys and possessions; I mean your investment assets, i.e., those assets that are being used to create wealth. If you can answer yes to this question, then your balance sheet is improving. If the answer is no, you are headed for trouble. If your answer is, What is a balance sheet? then you are already in trouble. You are like the ship ignoring the lighthouse and heading for danger.

Let me share with you a story to help you understand. This story comes from the Bible. The Bible is not only a great religious book, but it also has great nuggets of financial wisdom as well. Many people are familiar with the Old Testament story of Joseph who was sold into Egypt. While in Egypt, Joseph interpreted the dream of Pharaoh and told Pharaoh that Egypt would have seven years of plenty, followed by seven years of famine. Pharaoh then made Joseph a ruler of the land, including managing the financial affairs of Egypt.

This is where the financial lesson comes. Joseph gathered all the excess in the years of plenty and stored it. In other words, Joseph managed the balance sheet of Egypt by building up Egypt's food inventory. With a strong balance sheet, Egypt was prepared to weather the financial storm of the seven years of famine. When the seven years of famine did come, Egypt was prepared, and no one in Egypt went hungry. In fact, not only did the people of Egypt survive, but they thrived. During the famine years, people came from all over to buy food. Thus, because the balance sheet was effectively managed, not only did Egypt survive the famine, Egypt prospered during the famine. Think of that for a second: Egypt actually prospered because of the famine.

Manage your balance sheet. It will allow you to not only sleep when the financial storm blows, but also to thrive because of the storm.

Do Manage Your Risk
The fourth "Do" law of investing is to manage your risk. There are several ways to do this. An entire book could be written on this topic alone. In this chapter, I simply want to address two key points. First, that you understand your risk. Second, that you have a plan in place to manage that risk.

You cannot manage your risk if you do not know your risk. Risk comes in many forms. Many can be anticipated; many cannot. You must constantly ask yourself, What could possibly go wrong? Then, What can I do today to either make sure it does not go wrong or to at least mitigate the impact if it does go wrong?

For example, an oil company is in the business of producing oil. One obvious risk is: What happens if the price of oil suddenly plunges? This has happened before. A prudent chief financial officer will have thought this through. Generally, they hedge the price of oil, i.e., they agree to sell oil in the future based on the agreed upon price today. Then if the price of oil drops, they get to still sell their oil at the higher price. Of course, if the price of oil goes up, they still must sell the oil at the agreed upon price, thus losing out on that potential upside. In exchange for giving up some upside if the price of oil goes up, they reduce their risk of the price of oil going down.

I once had a discussion with the CEO of a publicly traded oil company. At the time, oil prices were steadily increasing. Many in the industry were not "hedging" their production because they wanted to capture the rising prices. He insisted that his company hedge some of their production. He got some pushback, and some perhaps even thought he was crazy, but he held firm. Oil prices later tanked. I think he now looks quite smart. He understood his risk and put a plan in place to reduce that risk.

Do you know what could go wrong in your financial life? Do you have a plan to deal with it?

Shortly after I graduated from university, I decided I wanted to invest in residential real estate. I found a duplex that I was able to buy directly from the builder for no money down. It seemed like a great deal. However, I looked at the risk and determined that if the duplex was vacant for a month or two, I would not be able to make the mortgage payment. Further, if the value dropped, and I had to sell for a loss, I did not have the capital to pay off the mortgage. To manage my risk, I went to a friend who was well-established in his professional career. He had the cash flow and the net worth to cover both of my risk scenarios. We agreed to buy the property together. I had found the investment and would manage the property. He would provide the capital and fund any mortgage payments and losses if there was insufficient cash.

Although I gave up some of the upside if the investment went well, I also eliminated any downside if the investment lost money. Manage your risk. Understand what it is, and then come up with a plan to manage it.

Key Takeaways:
The "Do" Laws of Investing are:
1. **Do Get a Little Richer Every Day.**
2. **Do Invest in Yourself through Education.**
3. **Do Build Your Balance Sheet.**
4. **Do Manage Your Risk.**

19

THE FOUR "DO NOT" LAWS OF INVESTING

Just as there are four "Do" laws of investing, there are also four "Do Not" laws of investing. The four "Do Not" laws are as follows:

1. Do Not Lose Money.
2. Do Not Invest What You Cannot Afford to Lose.
3. Do Not Be a Gambler.
4. Do Not Make Excuses.

Do Not Lose Money
The first "Do Not" law of investing is quite simple. (I wish I had understood it better when I was younger.) Do Not Lose Money. In other words, safety first. I know this sounds obvious, but too few investors consider this law before investing. Everybody likes to talk about their winning investments, but nobody talks about their losing investments. That is unfortunate, as there are plenty of losing investments. But because no one talks about them, people are lulled into a false sense of security that losing investments do not exist. They do exist, and they delay you from achieving financial freedom.

If every time you make an investment, you remind yourself that your first priority is to not lose money, you will make better investment decisions. In the previous chapter, I talked about bringing in an investor on a real estate transaction to manage my downside risk. I was applying the first "Do Not" law of investing. I was giving up some upside to eliminate the downside.

Manage your risk. Do everything you can to make sure you do not lose money. It sounds obvious, but many people forget to apply this principle.

Do Not Invest What You Cannot Afford to Lose
Even if you religiously apply the first law, Do Not Lose Money, the reality is sometimes you will. Nobody bats 1,000 in their investments. Nobody *never* makes a bad investment. Despite your best efforts, sometimes your investments, through no fault of your own, become worthless. You may have done absolutely everything perfectly, but uncontrollable circumstances happen, and the investment goes bad. That is why this second law is so important. Do not invest what you cannot afford to lose.

Every time you make an investment ask yourself, If this investment is entirely lost, will I be able to sleep at night? Will I still be financially okay? If the answer is no, do not make the investment. Every time you make an investment, you face the possibility that you could lose it all. Therefore, if you cannot afford to lose the investment, you should not make the investment.

As part of my plan to create passive income, I once made an investment in a publicly traded company that paid a regular dividend. The company operated in an industry I was familiar with. I did my research, I liked the company's business plan, I liked the sector it operated in, I liked the history of the company, and I liked that they were audited by one of the "Big Four" international audit firms, so I felt I could trust their financial information. After doing my due diligence, I felt comfortable investing, and so I did.

What I did not know was that the company's audited financial statements were fraudulent. Management had been deceiving their auditors, and their statements were not accurate. When the fraud was discovered, the company went bankrupt, and my investment became worthless. I felt I had done everything right, but I still lost my entire investment.

Fortunately, I had followed this law: Do not invest what you cannot afford to lose. I made sure that the size of the investment I made was something I could survive if I lost it all. So, while I was not happy about losing the entire investment, I did not lose any sleep over it. This experience drove home a simple lesson. If you cannot afford to lose it all, do not make the investment. I hope you can learn this lesson from my experience and not through your own experience. Personal experience is a very expensive teacher.

Buy the Milk First

Do Not Be a Gambler

The third "Do Not" law of investing is: Do not be a gambler. You are gambling when your investment goals are unrealistic, which is a polite way of saying you are being greedy. Too often people set unrealistic goals or expectations. They get big dollar signs in their eyes and lose all sense of reason. As they set unrealistic goals for themselves, they take on more risk. As they take on more risk, they violate the first "Do Not" law of investing: Do Not Lose Money. Keep your investment goals realistic. Do not expect to be an overnight success. Everybody knows about the person who was an overnight success and suddenly became very wealthy. However, the truth is behind every overnight success story, there are 15 years of hard work. Remember the power of compounding discussed in Chapter 16 and let that power work for you. If you do, you will find that your overall returns are better than if you are a gambler.

I had a friend who was looking into making an investment in a gold refining company. The gold refinery was based in a Caribbean country where the gold would be mined and then brought to a facility for refining. My friend asked me for my thoughts and if I would attend a presentation with him at the corporate office where they would provide more details. I agreed. The office was nicely finished and the presentation was professional. The presenters had personally visited the refinery and could attest to the refining process. The promised returns, though, were extraordinarily high. Everything seemed too unrealistic to me and threw up all sorts of red flags.

When I got home, I started doing some research and some basic calculations. What I learned was that for this company to provide the promised returns, the small facility in the Caribbean would have to refine close to the entire world's demand for gold. The investment was clearly a hoax. I shared the research, calculations, and conclusion with my friend. I told him I would not go near that investment. However, he saw dollar signs. He saw that he could make one simple investment so that he could retire, and he did not listen to me.

Rather, he took most of his money out of his retirement account and made the investment. He was looking for a get-rich-quick opportunity. No surprise that he lost it all. He gambled, and he lost. His financial situation and retirement plan would have vastly improved if he had simply followed this "Do Not" law of investing. It reminds me of an adage I heard long ago: "What happens when a man with money meets a man with experience?" Answer: "The man with experience ends up with the money, and the man with money ends up with the experience." Do not gain experience this way. Do not gamble.

One way that people gamble is by chasing highly speculative investments with their hard-earned capital. Although you may be tempted to do this, you can avoid it if you strictly adhere to two conditions.

First, only speculate after you have built up your foundation of wealth. Until then, be smart and take the sure path to financial freedom. If you choose this path, you will make better investment decisions, and with better investment decisions, you will see your wealth grow faster.

Second, only speculate using your investment or passive income; never speculate using your capital. This is the way you make sure you do not lose more than you can afford. A speculative investment is by its very nature highly speculative, meaning it has a high probability of becoming worthless. Thus, you need to plan for that. If you only speculate with what you are currently earning in passive income, then you are not putting your capital at risk. If the investment goes bad, you can replace that investment with next year's investment income. This means that you are not putting your financial security at risk. If you put more than that at risk, then you are being greedy.

If my friend would have at least acknowledged that his investment was speculative, and then followed this advice, he would have still been much better off. He would have made a smaller investment and still retained his capital. If the investment paid off, it still would have been life-changing. Even though he was gambling, he could have had the life-changing opportunity without the degree of risk he was taking.

Do Not Make Excuses

The fourth "Do Not" law of investing is: Do not make excuses. Plans will not always turn out perfectly. Mistakes will be made. When you make mistakes, do not compound the mistake by making excuses. Own the mistake and learn from the mistake. If something does not go well, sit back and honestly ask yourself, What went wrong? What could I have done differently? What can I learn from this mistake so I will be smarter and better? What can I learn from this mistake that will make me a better person or a better investor? If you do this, then your mistake is not wasted. Rather, it forms part of your education, and as I stated earlier, education is critically important.

I once had a great employee. He was intelligent, hard-working, and reliable. We worked on a large and complicated project together. He was my right-hand person and responsible for the project. We encountered many issues, and though we finally completed the project, I had to write off over $100,000. My employee knew that I took a huge write-off on the project. He felt responsible for the write-off, so he offered to resign.

I looked at him and basically said, "Are you crazy? I just invested over $100,000 in your education. Do you think I want you to resign so my competitor can get the benefit from that costly education? Just learn from it. I am sure those mistakes will never be made again."

It is okay to make mistakes; just learn from them. Otherwise, you have just paid for and wasted an excellent learning opportunity.

Key Takeaways:
The "Do Not" Laws of Investing are:
    1. Do Not Lose Money.
    2. Do Not Invest What You Cannot Afford to Lose.
    3. Do Not Be a Gambler.
    4. Do Not Make Excuses.

20

BUSINESS RELATIONSHIPS: HOW TO CHOOSE THEM, HOW TO KEEP THEM

As your investible assets grow, you will have opportunities to invest with other people. Someone might ask you to partner up with them or invest in their business. Alternatively, you might go to someone and ask them to partner up or invest with you. Such arrangements, if properly done, can be beneficial to all parties. However, this can also be a recipe for disaster. Make sure you understand what you are doing before entering any arrangements. Here are a few thoughts to consider:

Advantages
There are many advantages to partnering up with someone. One obvious advantage is complementary skill sets. A great business usually needs more than one skill set to be successful. If you have some, but not all, of the required skills, it may make sense to partner up with another individual. Each person bringing a unique and required skill set that the other party does not have.

Another advantage is capital. You may not have sufficient capital (or you may not want to invest the sufficient capital) to make the business a success. In this case, you can bring in one or more partners who pool their capital to ensure the business is a success.

Disadvantages

There are also several disadvantages. First, who gets what? When you invest with others, the equity and profits of the project must also be shared with others. Each partner will contribute (generally money, time, or expertise), and you must all agree on the relative value of each contribution and the associated equity from that value.

Another disadvantage of investing with others is that you introduce interpersonal dynamics. These interpersonal dynamics have ruined many friendships and many families. For example, Who controls? Who makes the decisions? Does a decision require unanimous support, or does just one person get to make all the decisions? Are the roles and responsibilities of each party clearly outlined? What happens if one person does not perform their agreed upon duties? What happens if the personal objectives of each party start to differ? What if one party wants to sell, but the other party does not? There are numerous questions that are best addressed upfront before they become a problem.

Integrity of Partners

The other aspect to consider is the integrity of your partner. A lack of integrity in your partner can cause you immeasurable grief. If, for any reason at all, you doubt the integrity or trustworthiness of your partner, do not walk away—run away. Your partner will only cause you heartache and grief. In business, there is no such thing as a "white lie." Anybody who will lie about small things will also lie about big things.

I once had a business manager send a presentation to me and my partner about our competitors. The presentation was well done, informative, and even entertaining. However, there was one small item in the presentation that seemed off. Totally insignificant in terms of importance but still bothersome, as it indicated a small deception was occurring. I said to my partner that anyone who will deceive us about something this small will also deceive us about bigger things.

We started doing a more thorough background check, so we called the university where the business manager claimed he graduated from. They had no record of him. (And they checked thoroughly. Universities take misrepresented degrees very seriously.) We made some other calls about his background and found out it was also fabricated. Turns out, his resume was a fraud. When confronted, he admitted to the deceptions, and we had to fire him on the spot. You cannot work with people you cannot trust. The potential upside of working with an untrustworthy partner will never offset the potential downside. If they are not trustworthy, you should not invest together.

Where There Is Smoke, There Is Fire
If in doing your due diligence or vetting other people, you find a few loose ends that you are not quite comfortable with, take those as red flags. My experience has been that where there is smoke, there is fire. You are much better off to not do a deal than to do a bad deal. If you are not comfortable with the other person, it is, by definition, a bad deal.

I once represented a group of investors in a real estate transaction. While representing them, I was introduced to an individual who represented a company that wanted to enter a joint venture to develop the property. He was an extremely charming and likeable individual. However, during our first meeting, he said a couple of things that did not seem quite right or consistent with what I knew. Red flags immediately went up in my mind that I could not trust this person, and I refused to establish a joint venture with him. I was later proven correct, as this person went on to cause a significant amount of grief, including alleged stealing and falsifying documents.

Trust your instincts. If you notice smoke, you can assume there is a fire. It is much better to walk away than to get involved with less scrupulous people. The same principle applies when looking at numbers. If the numbers do not make sense and if the projected return is too high, these are indicators that something is wrong. Do your extra due diligence, and if you don't feel comfortable, do not walk away—run away. The imminent pain and grief are not worth the potential reward.

Write It Down
Even after having done all your due diligence and having chosen a trustworthy co-investor, things can still go wrong. When this happens, people's recollections are often different. This is what causes friendships and families

to be torn apart. If you are going to invest with someone, make sure there is a clear understanding of everything and write it down.

Writing it down is beneficial for three reasons:

1. It forces people to think things through a little deeper and with a little more clarity.
2. It reduces the chance of a misunderstanding. Everyone can read the document and agree that the document reflects the intent of all parties.
3. Down the road, if there is ever any disagreement, everyone can go back to the document and see what was agreed upon. While writing it down does not guarantee there will never be disagreements, it certainly reduces the chances.

Writing it down is critically important, especially if it is family. If you want to make sure your familial relationships survive, write it down. I am aware of situations where family members co-invested; they all trusted each other and did not think it was worth the effort or cost to write it all down. Years later, they all regretted it. Disagreements arose and there was no mechanism to resolve the differences. This is what causes friendships and families to break up.

If you value your relationships, particularly your familial relationships, and you choose to invest together, write it down.

Key Takeaways:
1. **Investing with others has advantages and disadvantages. Understand both before investing with others.**
2. **Only invest with those who are trustworthy.**
3. **Make sure all arrangements are written down, particularly family arrangements.**

21

RETIREMENT: ARE YOU FINANCIALLY READY?

If you follow the advice in this book, you will reach the stage when you are able to retire. However, this can sometimes be a scary step. How do you know if you are financially ready to retire?

I suggest a simple three-step approach:

1. Calculate your burn rate
2. Calculate your passive income
3. Test your retirement plan

The first step in testing if you are ready to retire is to calculate your "burn rate." By burn rate, I mean the amount of money each year that you spend or "burn." This should be straightforward, as it should come right off your personal income statement (which you should be an expert at by now).

The next step is to calculate your passive income. What will your income be when you cease working? This should also be straightforward, but it may be mildly more complicated than calculating your family burn rate. Your passive income will be your existing passive income that you have built up, plus any other income sources you may be getting, such as a company pension or government pension.

The final step is to test your retirement plan. Once you have estimated your burn rate and your passive income, you are ready to test yourself. Give yourself a final exam for retirement readiness. Test yourself to see if your calculations are accurate or if you may have missed something.

To do this, set up a separate bank account (or use an existing one) and only deposit the amount of money your calculations say will be your burn rate. Then live your life normally and pay all your bills from that one account. Do this for a couple of years.

If you find that at the end of each year you were able to easily maintain your lifestyle out of the funds you put into that one account, congratulations! You are ready to retire, and you have proven that your passive income sources will allow you to maintain your lifestyle. If you find that your bank account runs out of money, then you know that your burn rate is higher than you anticipated, and you will need to recalculate.

There are three ways to solve this problem:

1. You can reduce expenses. After you retire, some of your expenses may go down (of course, others may go up). Have you properly accounted for these potential changes?
2. You can increase income. You can continue to work and build up your passive income.
3. You can use your capital. Many financial advisors do their projections, assuming every year a certain amount of your capital will be drawn down and used to support your current living expenses. (And 4% of capital is a commonly referred to number.) While this is certainly doable, it makes me nervous. Every time I draw down capital, I also reduce my future passive income. Further, I do not know how much longer I am going to live and therefore how much capital I am going to need. If I start drawing down my capital, my fear is that I will run out of capital before I run out of time. Thus, while this is an option, it is not the one I personally use.

I performed this test for several years before I retired. Every month, I would deposit into my account the amount of money I thought I needed to pay all my family bills. It was a "final exam" of my budget. Could I really live on my budget? What I learned was that each year my actual expenditures were remarkably close to my budget. That gave me the confidence to know that my passive income was sufficient to cover my family burn rate.

Buy the Milk First

When I got tired of working full-time, I was confident to make the change. I had already been living on my "retirement income" and knew that it would be sufficient to cover my burn rate. I suggest you do the same. Learn to live off your retirement income before you retire. This will give you the confidence to know you can retire and still live the lifestyle you want. It will also eliminate a lot of stress by avoiding the mistake of retiring too soon and discovering your lifestyle needs more income. Make sure your budget can pass its "final exam" before you take that step to retire.

Key Takeaway:
1. **Test your retirement readiness. Before you retire, only live off your projected retirement income.**

PART V

PASSING ON THE PLAN

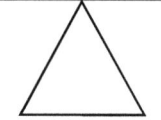

22

LENDING TO FAMILY AND FRIENDS

As you start to accumulate wealth, family and friends will come and ask you to loan them money. Despite my previous comments that money is a tool that should be used to improve lives, let me share some thoughts regarding loaning money to family and friends.

Loaning money to family and friends is not always the best way to improve lives.

First, ask yourself, Can I afford to loan? If your assets are such that you cannot afford to lose the money that you are loaning, then you cannot afford to offer the loan. That makes the answer easy. Simply explain to the person that you are not currently in a position that allows you to loan. You do not have to explain further, and do not let them pressure you. If you succumb to pressure that means you are letting a lower priority take precedence over a higher priority and remember that should never be done.

Second, when you are considering loaning to family or friends, understand that you should never loan that which you would not be willing to give. By that I mean, ask yourself one simple yet important question, Am I prepared to offer this as a gift? If the answer is no, then do not consider a loan. Loans go bad. Even honourable people who have every intention of repaying you sometimes cannot repay the loan. If that happens, you will have effectively made it a gift. If you are not prepared to offer a gift, then do not offer the loan as you may be forced to provide a gift that you otherwise would not have made. Then ill feelings develop. When ill feelings develop, you can ruin a valued relationship. Thus, ask yourself, Am I prepared to lose this relationship? If the answer is no, then you only have two options: 1) do not make the loan or 2) make the loan but tell yourself it is a gift. Then if the "gift" gets repaid you are grateful, but if the "gift" does not get repaid, that is okay too because in your mind it was never a loan—it was always a gift.

Third, even if you can afford to loan, and you are willing to provide this gift, it still may not be the right path to take. You need to ask yourself a few more questions. Questions such as, Why is the money needed? Am I truly helping them, or am I enabling them?

For example, if they have not learned how to manage money (they are controlled by money as opposed to controlling the money), will loaning money or even giving them money make their problems go away? Probably not. This is because their lack of money is not the real problem. The real problem is their lack of ability to manage money. Thus, in this situation, giving them money is not helpful. It will not teach them the financial laws they need to know to truly solve their problems. Rather, it will enable and mask the real problem, which often creates even worse financial problems. If this is the situation, ask yourself if you can help in a different way. Can you help them find extra work so they can earn what they need? Can you assist them in developing their own budget? Teach them the principles discussed in this book. Help them understand the financial laws they are not applying because, if followed, it will solve their problems. This way, you are not only helping them solve their financial problems, but you are also setting them up for success.

Further, you will also be giving them a stronger sense of accountability, and more importantly, you are helping them gain confidence. Perhaps you can even pay for a financial planner who will teach them how to manage money. If you give money to someone who has not learned how to manage their finances, then you are not helping. You are hurting. You are enabling, and you are promoting a life of financial servitude.

There is an old saying that applies here: "If you give a man a fish, you feed him for a day; if you teach a man to fish, you feed him for life." If someone is coming to you for money, the more charitable act may not be to give them a fish, rather it could be to teach them to fish. Though it may not appear so to your friend or family member, teaching them to fish is usually a more charitable act, yet a more difficult act. Analyze the situation and determine the actual needs—not what they think they need. Sometimes it is money, but sometimes it is teaching.

I once had a couple of individuals call me up, wondering if I could loan them some money. I knew these individuals well. I also knew their background and that they had never learned how to manage money. I knew they were calling me, looking for the easy way to solve their problems. I told them I would be happy to talk with them, so I invited them to come by my house. I am sure they came by expecting some money. However, I did not give them money. Rather, I sat them down and gave them a basic lesson on budgeting. I asked them to work through their income and expenses and then to come back to me with a budget, along with a more specific request as to what their needs were. I told them to take a couple of weeks to pull this information together and then to give me a call so we could get together again. They were very polite and were grateful for my time. But I never heard from them again (at least with respect to money).

They wanted a fish, but instead I tried to teach them to fish. Their money problems obviously were not as serious as they indicated; otherwise, they would have called me back. My suspicions are they found an easier short-term solution. By offering to teach them to fish I was offering a more difficult, but long-term solution.

Fourth, if after considering all the above, you are still inclined to offer a loan, my advice is to write it down. When dealing with financial matters, especially when it involves family and friends, write it down. Make all the expectations clear. How much are you loaning? When will it be repaid? What interest rate is being charged? What happens if the loan is not paid? Treat it as though you were two totally independent parties making a business transaction. That way, there is no misunderstanding of the terms and expectations. Writing it down will help preserve the relationship.

Key Takeaways:
When loaning money to family and friends:
1. **Make sure you can afford it.**
2. **Never loan that which you would not be willing to offer as a gift.**
3. **Make sure you are not enabling poor money management.**
4. **Teach them to fish; do not give them a fish.**
5. **Write it down.**

23

MONEY IS ONLY A SYMBOL

If you have followed the principles in this book, you have learned how to control your finances, rather than be controlled. You have learned some basic financial laws that will enrich your life and lead you to prosperity. Now for a few general comments.

First, understand that money is only a symbol. It is a medium of exchange. Money, in and of itself, is worthless. It is only worth what we, as a collective society, decide it is worth and what we are willing to exchange it for.

Back in Chapter 10, I said that you should never let a lower priority take precedence over a higher priority. This statement is universal, and it applies here too. Do not let money take precedence over higher priorities. Understand what money is, and what money is not. Money is not the most important thing in life. Money should not drive all decisions. Money is not the root of all evil. However, the *love of money* is the root of evil. When money is loved more than everything else, then a lower priority has taken precedence over higher priorities, and that is never good. Do not love money more than everything else. Understand that money is a tool. It is a tool that should be used to improve life. Use money to improve your life, the life of your family members, and the life of others. Money is not something to be hoarded or locked away in a vault where it can do no good. Understand what is important.

I grew up in a family of five children. My only sister is the eldest sibling, followed by four boys—we were always active as young boys. In our backyard, we had a swing set. We would play on the swing set, but in so doing, we destroyed the grass underneath. One day, my mom complained to my dad that we were ruining the grass. My dad looked at my mom and said, "I am not raising grass. I am raising boys." That was the last time my mom worried about the grass. My parents had their priorities right. They understood their boys were more important than the grass. The grass could always be replaced. The boys could not.

I remember another time I was driving my parents' car when I got rear-ended and caused a lot of damage to the car. When I got home, my mom phoned my dad to let him know I had been in an accident with the car. The very first thing my dad asked was, "Is Murray okay?" He did not care about the car. The car was a physical possession that could be replaced. He cared about me. I was blessed with parents who understood money was a tool. While they worked hard and experienced financial success, they always put people over possessions, and because they did, they had much more joy in their lives. Learn from my parents' example. Do not let the love of money become the highest priority in your life. Use money as a tool to improve lives. You will be much happier if you do.

Key Takeaways:
1. **Do not let money take precedence over higher priorities.**
2. **Put people over possessions.**
3. **Use money as a tool to improve lives.**

24

MONEY CAN BUY HAPPINESS

There is an old saying, "Money can't buy happiness." I disagree. Money can buy happiness—if you spend it right. The pursuit of wealth is not evil. However, placing the pursuit of wealth above all else is. I cannot emphasize enough the importance of understanding priorities. Nor can I emphasize enough the need to never let a lower priority take precedence over a higher priority. If you have pursued wealth above all else, you have paid too steep a price. Relationships, family, integrity, and many other values are all much higher priorities than wealth.

As previously stated, the belief that money is the root of all evil is wrong. It is the *love of money* that is the root of all evil. Why is that? Because when the love of money is placed as the highest priority, evil sets in. As discussed in the previous chapter, money is a tool. If you use this tool correctly by blessing the lives of others, then money *can* buy happiness. Many philanthropists have stated that giving away money is much more enjoyable than earning it. If you have been fortunate enough to create sufficient wealth for your needs, consider using your wealth to bless others. You will be glad you did.

There is more than one religion that teaches about paying a tithe. A tithe is 10% of your income. I encourage everyone, regardless of their religion, to pay a tithe. In fact, a tithe should be a fixed expense and the first thing you pay. I pay at least a tithe to my church every year. I have done so for as long as I can remember. I have never regretted it. I believe I am a richer person because of it, and I believe you will be a richer person too. Money can buy happiness. It all just depends on how you spend it.

Key Takeaways:
1. **Money can buy happiness.**
2. **Money is not the root of all evil. The *love of money* is.**
3. **Use money as a tool to bless others.**
4. **Pay a tithe.**

25

CONCLUSION

If you have made it this far, congratulations! I hope you have enjoyed reading this book as much as I have enjoyed writing it. You are well on your path to getting your financial house in order. However, reading this book is not enough. You must understand and apply the principles discussed in this book.

In summary, it really is all about the 3 Ps. You simply need to plan. You need to determine where you want to be and when you want to be there. Then you need to determine what steps you need to take to get there. Next, prioritize. Decide what is important to you and rank those priorities. Never let a lower priority take precedence over a higher priority. Never. This part is surprisingly logical, yet surprisingly difficult. Stay focused on your higher priorities. Finally, perform. You need to act. Failure to act makes the first two steps just wishes. Performing, or acting, is what yields results. The tools and concepts discussed in this book should help you plan, prioritize, and perform. In other words, they will help you to always buy the milk first. If you do this, I promise you will prosper and you will be able to sleep when the financial wind blows.

Finally, one parting comment. Once you get it all figured out financially and start generating the results you want, there is a fourth P. Pay it forward. Pass on the plan. Help others. That is where the real joy is found.

Key Takeaways:
   1. In summary, it is all about the 3 Ps.
      a. Plan
      b. Prioritize
      c. Perform
   2. Buy the milk first.
   3. Once you get it all figured out, remember the fourth P.
      a. Pay it forward.

For more information and help go to

www.buythemilkfirst.com

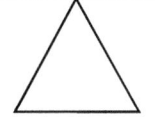

Appendix 1

SUMMARY OF KEY TAKEAWAYS

Chapter 1: Wealth Is Not a Number
1. Wealth is defined first by time—not money—and second by lifestyle.

Chapter 2: The Law of the Harvest
Remember the Law of the Harvest:
1. If you don't sow, you don't reap.
2. You reap only what has been sown.
3. You reap in a different season than you sow.
4. You reap more than you sow.
5. There is a direct correlation between the size of the harvest and the size of the effort.

Chapter 3: Natural Laws Can Be neither Broken nor Cheated
1. Financial laws, like natural laws, can be neither broken nor cheated.
2. Financial wisdom is the product of applying the knowledge of financial laws with the understanding of the consequences of those laws.

Chapter 4: Sleep When the Wind Blows
1. Success is a product of the 3 Ps. Plan, Prioritize, Perform.
2. Success is the difference between wishing and performing.

Chapter 5: Plan Your Financial Future
Plan your future. Ask yourself the following:
1. Where do I see myself in 1 year, 10 years, 20 years, and 30 years?
2. What steps do I have to take to get there?
3. Am I happy with the life balance I will create when I take those steps?

Chapter 6: Own Your Mistakes
1. Be flexible.
2. Own your mistakes.

Chapter 7: Plan for the Worst, Hope for the Best
1. Plan for the worst, hope for the best.
2. Have a will.
3. Keep your spouse fully informed on all family finances.

Chapter 8: A "Four-Letter Word" for Freedom
1. The prerequisite to a smart decision is an informed decision.
2. The better the information, the better the decision.
3. Creating a budget creates informed decisions.
4. Creating a budget must be a priority.

Chapter 9: The "Is" and the "Is Not"
1. Creating a budget must be a priority.
2. Budgeting allows you to take control of your finances, as opposed to having your finances control you.
3. When you find yourself in a financial hole, quit digging.
4. Budgeting allows you to take control of your emotions and thereby reduce the stress in your life.
5. You are free to make any choices you want, but you are not free from the consequences of your choices.

Chapter 10: Buy the Milk First
1. Prioritize your list of wants and needs.
2. Never, never, never let a lower priority take precedence over a higher priority. Never.

Chapter 11: The Rule of Financial Happiness

Live by the Rule of Financial Happiness:
1. Establish your fiscal priorities.
2. Determine your cash inflows.
3. Determine your cash outflows.
4. Adjust your cash inflows and outflows such that . . .
    a. Cash inflows are greater than cash outflows.
    b. Cash outflows match your priorities.

Chapter 12: Doing What You Want with What You Got

1. Build a budget that aligns with your goals.
2. Pay yourself first.
3. Put money into a short-term emergency fund.
4. Put money into a long-term investment fund.

Chapter 13: Help! I Am Short of Funds

To balance your budget:
1. Reduce Expenses.
2. Increase Income.
3. Change Lifestyle.

Chapter 14: Debt: The Good, the Bad, and the Ugly

1. Debt is a horrible master.
2. Get out of debt as soon as you can.
3. Avoid ugly debt at all costs.
4. Bad and ugly debts are the slayers of wealth and the mother of tears.

Chapter 15: Help! I Am Already in Debt

1. Calculate Your "Real Debt."
2. Create a Debt Calendar.
3. Attack the Debt.

Chapter 16: The Dynamic Duo—Secrets to Wealth Creation
1. Net investible income is the single most important factor in wealth creation.
2. Compounding is an incredibly powerful force that acts as a multiplier to net investible income.
3. Net investible income, combined with compounding, forms an unbeatable and life-changing Dynamic Duo.
4. The sooner you create net investible income, the more powerful is the multiplying force of compounding.

Chapter 17: Your Financial Personal Flotation Device
The *3 Be's* of Investing:
1. Be Patient—remember the "Bus Principle."
2. Be Focused.
3. Be Diligent.

Chapter 18: The Four "Do" Laws of Investing
The "Do" Laws of Investing are:
1. Do Get a Little Richer Every Day.
2. Do Invest in Yourself through Education.
3. Do Build Your Balance Sheet.
4. Do Manage Your Risk.

Chapter 19: The Four "Do Not" Laws of Investing
The "Do Not" Laws of Investing are:
1. Do Not Lose Money.
2. Do Not Invest What You Cannot Afford to Lose.
3. Do Not Be a Gambler.
4. Don Not Make Excuses.

Chapter 20: Business Relationships: How to Choose Them, How to Keep Them

1. Investing with others has advantages and disadvantages. Understand both before investing with others.
2. Only invest with those who are trustworthy.
3. Make sure all arrangements are written down, particularly family arrangements.

Chapter 21: Retirement: Are You Financially Ready?

1. Test your retirement readiness. Before you retire, only live off your projected retirement income.

Chapter 22: Lending to Family and Friends

When loaning money to family and friends:
1. Make sure you can afford it.
2. Never loan that which you would not be willing to offer as a gift.
3. Make sure you are not enabling poor money management.
4. Teach them to fish; do not give them a fish.
5. Write it down.

Chapter 23: Money Is Only a Symbol

1. Do not let money take precedence over higher priorities.
2. Put people over possessions.
3. Use money as a tool to improve lives.

Chapter 24: Money Can Buy Happiness

1. Money can buy happiness.
2. Money is not the root of all evil. The *love of money* is.
3. Use money as a tool to bless others.
4. Pay a tithe.

Chapter 25: Conclusion
1. In summary, it is all about the 3 Ps.
    a. Plan
    b. Prioritize
    c. Perform
2. Buy the milk first.
3. Once you get it all figured out, remember the fourth P.
    a. Pay it forward.

About the Author

Murray J Lee is an accredited accountant (CPA) with over thirty years of public practice experience including twenty years as a partner at two different international "Big Four" accounting firms. He graduated with both a Bachelor and a Masters-in-Accounting from Brigham Young University. Aside from his entrepreneurial involvement in various retail, real estate, hotel and restaurant ventures, he has been on the Board of numerous tax-exempt entities and currently sits on the Board as the Lead Director of a NASDAQ and TSX listed public corporation. He is happily married to his wife Leslie with whom he shares five children and twenty grandchildren. This book was written for them.

CPSIA information can be obtained
at www.ICGtesting.com
Printed in the USA
BVHW041316260422
635365BV00017B/1395

9 781039 122048